T&T CLARK STUDY GUIDES TO THE OLD TESTAMENT

1 & 2 KINGS

Series Editor
Adrian Curtis, University of Manchester, UK

Published in Association with the Society for Old Testament Study

1 & 2 KINGS
AN INTRODUCTION AND STUDY GUIDE

HISTORY AND STORY IN ANCIENT ISRAEL

By
Lester L. Grabbe

Bloomsbury T&T Clark
An imprint of Bloomsbury Publishing Plc

B L O O M S B U R Y
LONDON · OXFORD · NEW YORK · NEW DELHI · SYDNEY

Bloomsbury T&T Clark

An imprint of Bloomsbury Publishing Plc

Imprint previously known as T&T Clark

50 Bedford Square	1385 Broadway
London	New York
WC1B 3DP	NY 10018
UK	USA

www.bloomsbury.com

BLOOMSBURY, T&T CLARK and the Diana logo are trademarks of Bloomsbury Publishing Plc

First published 2017

British Library Cataloguing-in-Publication Data
A catalogue record for this book is available from the British Library.

ISBN:	PB:	978-0-56767-085-4
	ePDF:	978-0-56767-086-1
	ePUB:	978-0-56767-087-8

Library of Congress Cataloging-in-Publication Data
A catalog record for this book is available from the Library of Congress.

Cover design by clareturner.co.uk

Typeset by Forthcoming Publications (www.forthpub.com)
Printed and bound in Great Britain

CONTENTS

Chapter 6

CHAPTER

ABBREVIATIONS

AB	Anchor Bible
ABD	*Anchor Bible Dictionary*
AfO	*Archiv für Orientforschung*
BASOR	*Bulletin of the American Schools of Oriental Research*
BBB	Bonner biblische Beiträge
BZAW	Beiheft to *Zeitschrift für die alttestamentliche Wissenschaft'*
CBQM	*Catholic Biblical Quarterly*, Monograph Series
CBR	*Currents in Biblical Research*
DH	Deuteronomistic History
DtrH	Deuteronomistic Historian
ESHM	European Seminar in Historical Methodology
FAT	Forschungen zum Alten Testament
FOTL	Forms of Old Testament Literature
HdO	Handbuch der Orientalistik
HSM	Harvard Semitic Monographs
IEJ	*Israel Exploration Journal*
JAOS	*Journal of the American Oriental Society*
JBL	*Journal of Biblical Literature*
JSOT	*Journal for the Study of the Old Testament*
JSOTSup	*Journal for the Study of the Old Testament*, Supplement Series
LCL	Loeb Classical Library
LHBOTS	Library of Hebrew Bible/Old Testament Studies
NCB	New Century Bible
OBO	Orbus biblicus et orientalis
OLA	Orientalia lovaniensia analecta
OTL	Old Testament Library
OTS	*Oudtestamentische Studiën*
SBLSymS	Society of Biblical Literature Symposium Series
SHANE	Studies in the History of the Ancient Near East
SHCANE	Studies in the History and Culture of the Ancient Near East
TA	*Tel Aviv*
UF	*Ugarit-Forschungen*
VT	*Vetus Testamentum*
VTSup	*Vetus Testamentum*, Supplements
WBC	Word Bible Commentary
ZAW	*Zeitschrift für die alttestamentliche Wissenschaft*
ZDPV	*Zeitschrift des Deutschen Palästina-Vereins*

Chapter 1

INTRODUCTION

Apart from Genesis and perhaps the story of David in 1 and 2 Samuel, the stories in the books of Kings are some of the best known to the broader public. This is a good place to start for the person wanting to begin studying the Bible seriously, especially with the aim of learning how a section of the text has been analyzed and commented on by professional scholars of the Bible.

Corresponding to the aims of the series in which it appears, this short volume intends to give guidance on the scholarship of the books of 1 and 2 Kings to the reader, especially to the student and others who are new to or less experienced in the subject. Each volume in the series takes an approach suitable to the subject of the biblical book in question and the aims of the author. In the case of the present volume a number of methods have been applied by scholarship to the books of 1 and 2 Kings through the centuries. One particular approach cannot be pursued to the exclusion of all others, but there has definitely been a concentration of studies on specific aspects of the biblical books of Kings over the years. It is the popular approach of *historiography* that will occupy the largest amount of space, but it is hoped that readers will find other approaches discussed here that might interest them and sufficient bibliography to follow them up in future study.

In this introductory chapter we shall explore some of the issues that affect the interpretation of 1 and 2 Kings, before concentrating on a few key ones in the rest of the book. This will include the questions of the text, various methods of interpretation, and the issue of historiography in relation to the books of Kings.

Interpreting the Books of Kings

There is no doubt that the books of Kings contain memorable stories: Solomon and the queen of Sheba, Elijah and Elisha, Ahab and Jezebel, the siege and fall of Samaria to the Assyrians, Hezekiah and the Sennacherib invasion, the alleged sins of Manasseh, the cult reform of Josiah, Zedekiah and the final days of Jerusalem. What is their function? Were they meant as history? Were they just written and preserved as entertainment? Were they ancient Israelite literature? Were they lessons in morality and theology? All of these questions are relevant and suggest method-ologies that have been applied to our two books. Textual criticism will be discussed later in the present chapter. Form and source criticism are dealt with in Chapter 2. Theology will be discussed in the final chapter (Chapter 6), along with several hermeneutical methods, such as feminist criticism and postcolonialism.

In spite of all these different methods of studying the books, when modern readers of the Bible engage with 1 and 2 Kings, the first thought likely to come to mind is that this is history—history of the kings of Israel. Of course, the first two kings, according to the biblical narrative, were Saul and David, and their story is told mostly in 1 and 2 Samuel. But the story of David ends in 1 Kings 1, with the account of how Solomon was crowned king. As we shall discuss below, this makes use of the common concept of history rather than an academic one. It remains to be discussed whether 1 and 2 Kings are history as a modern historian would define and describe it.

The Text of 1 and 2 Kings

The foundation of exegesis is textual criticism. In order to interpret, one must have a text to interpret. The original aim of textual criticism was to get back to the 'original text'. This of course assumes that there was an original text, whereas many contemporary interpreters would doubt the existence of a single original text for many writings. This is because many Jewish writings are community products, rather than being the creation of a single author who wrote and finalized and promulgated an original and final form of the text. Nevertheless, it is important to understand the history of the text, and many scholars want to reach as early a stage in the textual growth as possible.

The traditional Hebrew text of Kings is referred to as the *Masoretic text* (MT), after the medieval textual scribes called *Masoretes*. A Greek translation had been made at an early time, perhaps in the second century BCE for 1 and 2 Kings. This is often known as the *Septuagint* (LXX) or *Old Greek*. The Hebrew and Greek versions of Kings frequently differ from one another, sometimes in minor ways but occasionally in more significant ways (for an introduction to the various Greek versions, see Dines 2004). The biblical textual finds among the Dead Sea Scrolls have demonstrated that the Greek text had often been translated from a Hebrew text that differed from the traditional Jewish Hebrew text. In other words, the Greek translation differed from the Masoretic Hebrew text not because of translation considerations (misunderstandings, difficulties in rendering Hebrew into Greek, words or expressions not known by the translators, etc.) but because the Hebrew text underlying the LXX differed from the MT. Thus, when we look at 1 and 2 Kings, we need to be aware that where the Greek text differs from the traditional Jewish text (MT), this is probably not because of a translation issue but because it was based on a Hebrew text—now apparently lost—that differed. Yet some Jewish writers and exegetes had no hesitation in using the LXX text. After all, the Greek text was also a Jewish text, even if Christians later picked it up and used it.

A study of both the Hebrew and Greek texts of Samuel and Kings show that the texts of these books share a considerable history. Already a century ago Henry St John Thackeray (1921, 16-28) divided into five parts the Greek text of Samuel and Kings in the Vaticanus manuscript (which is one of the main witnesses to the Greek text). This textual division is different from the normal division of the Greek text into four books of 1–4 Kingdoms, with 1–2 Kingdoms roughly corresponding to 1 and 2 Samuel, and 3–4 Kingdoms with 1 and 2 Kings in the Hebrew text. Thackeray used the first four letters of the Greek alphabet (which are α, β, γ, δ) to designate the various sections of the Greek Kingdoms. This may seem confusing to a modern reader, but his designation is still often referred to in textual discussions:

α	1 Kingdoms (Antiochian)	(= 1 Samuel)
ββ	2 Kgdms 1–9 (Antiochian)	(= 2 Sam. 1–9)
βγ	2 Kgdms 10 to 3 Kgdms 2.11 (*kaige*)	(= 2 Sam. 10 to 1 Kgs 2.11)
γγ	3 Kgdms 2.12–21.43 (Antiochian)	(= 1 Kgs 2.12–21.29)
γδ	3 Kgdms 22.1 to 4 Kgdms 25.30 (*kaige*)	(= 1 Kgs 22.1 to 2 Kgs 25.30)

The latest scholarship has found different textual versions in these different sections. Two sections turn out to have a Greek text based closely on a text similar to the Masoretic text (βγ and γδ). This text is now known in scholarship as the *kaige* text or recension (based on the translation of the Hebrew particle *gam* by Greek *kaige*). This text or something very similar has also been identified in the fragments of the Greek translation of Theodotion, some quotations in the New Testament, and the Greek version of the Minor Prophets found among the Dead Sea Scrolls (Barthélemy 1963).

The bulk of the Greek text of 1 and 2 Kings, however, follows what is called the Antiochian or Lucianic text. This is named after the patristic writers around Antioch who used it, or after the Christian martyr Lucian who was associated with it. This text has been identified in a group of Greek manuscripts, in the Greek text that lies behind the Old Latin, and in Josephus' version of Samuel and Kings. The fragments of Samuel and Kings from Qumran, where they are extant, are also often said to agree closely with the Antiochian or Lucianic text (see Cross et al. 2005; Ulrich 1978). (Because of the general similarity of the texts, some observations on the Hebrew text of Samuel found at Qumran [4QSam^{a-c}] can be extrapolated to the text of Kings, even though little of the text of Kings has been preserved among the Dead Sea Scrolls.) What this demonstrates is that there was originally more than one *Hebrew* version of the text of Samuel and Kings.

The Lucianic text of 3 and 4 Kingdoms (1 and 2 Kings) in the LXX differs from the Hebrew in many small points, though these seldom affect the overall sense. We also find a different order of material at various points. For example, the story of Naboth's vineyard (1 Kgs 21; 3 Kgdms 20) occurs before the siege of Samaria by Ben-Hadad (1 Kgs 20; 3 Kgdms 21). Here are some other passages in which there are major differences between the Lucianic text and the MT:

3 Kingdoms 2.35a-o: this is a long addition (often called a 'plus') at this point in the Lucianic text (which would be 1 Kgs 2.35 in the MT) about the beginning of Solomon's reign: his wisdom, marriage to Pharaoh's daughter, and building activities. (All the details here are in fact also to be found in MT but in other passages.)

3 Kingdoms 2.46a-l: this is a textual plus with information on Solomon's household, table provisions, officials, and chariotry. Again, although the MT lacks this specific section at 1 Kgs 2.46, all the information is found elsewhere in the text of the MT.

3 Kingdoms 5.1-4: this corresponds to 1 Kgs 4.20–5.8, but several of the verses in the MT are lacking in the LXX and there is a slightly different order of material.

3 Kingdoms 12.24a-z: this textual plus in the Lucianic text of the LXX gives an alternative version of Jeroboam's rise to power, the death of his son, and the splitting of the kingdom. Yet all the material found here is also found elsewhere in the MT (such as at 1 Kgs 14.1-18). This passage was investigated by Zipora Talshir (1993). She concludes that the creator of the story had before him a version of 1 Kings similar to our present Hebrew text and that the alternative story is the writer's own creation made by rewriting and rearranging material from MT 1 Kings. Therefore, in her opinion it does not represent an independent tradition. This is a moot point. It could also be argued that this represents an independent tradition about Jeroboam's rise and was available in a Hebrew version to the translator of 3 Kgdms 12.24. Unfortunately, no such Hebrew version is currently extant, though Talshir makes a good case for reconstructing a Hebrew text as the *Vorlage* of the Greek text (i.e. the Hebrew original text from which the Greek text was translated). If independent, as already noted, the material it contains still does not differ in essentials from the story in the MT.

4 Kingdoms 10.37-43: this is a textual plus in the Lucianic text, absent from 2 Kgs 10.37. It is similar to MT 2 Kgs 8.25-29 and 9.27-28, though even here there are some greater or lesser differences.

Still to be determined is what the original LXX text was like. Some will argue that the original Greek text was more or less the same as the Lucianic, but others disagree. This is a matter still in debate among specialists. But whatever the exact original of the Greek text, it seems clear that it was translated from a Hebrew text different from the MT. Many would also argue that it was a text generally superior in quality to the MT.

The Books of Kings and Israelite Prophetic Activity

One topic that I shall raise here is the importance of the books of Kings for our understanding of prophets and prophecy in ancient Israel. For an understanding of this topic, there is a tendency to focus on the prophetic literature, the so-called Latter Prophets (i.e. the Major and Minor Prophets), but while these are obviously vital, the significance of the books of Samuel and Kings is often overlooked. Although the prophetic books give us written prophecies (that may or may not have been spoken orally), an actual description of prophets is often missing. On the other hand, the Former Prophets (1 and 2 Samuel; 1 and 2 Kings) show us the supposed actions of a number of prophets, especially Elijah and Elisha, but also Micaiah and Huldah and even Isaiah in Kings (a number of prophetic figures are of course known from 1 and 2 Samuel).

It is surprising how much of the text in 1 and 2 Kings revolves around prophetic figures. Most of the last part of 1 Kings (reign of Ahab: 1 Kgs 17–21) and the first part of 2 Kings (2 Kgs 1–9)—a textual stretch of 14 chapters—is mostly about the prophets Elijah and Elisha. What we call *prophetic legends* (on these, see Chapter 2, p. 20) are a major feature of 1 and 2 Kings. In addition to Elijah and Elisha, Isaiah also features prominently. In the story of Hezekiah's reign Isaiah is an essential part of the story; indeed, these chapters from 2 Kings found their way into the book of Isaiah as duplicates (2 Kgs 18.17–19.37//Isa. 36.1–37.38). Although there are a few other passages in the book of Isaiah that show Isaiah in action, the prophet is an important actor during the crisis of the Assyrian invasion under Hezekiah.

As we shall be discussing, the question of whether the individuals in the story did what the text says they did is often a complicated one. Nevertheless, our knowledge of how Israelite prophets acted depends on the picture of their activities in the biblical text. These descriptions might be stereotyped or imaginary in some cases, but prophets were known in ancient Israelite society. Even if the writer is giving a fictional account, he may well be describing something that he has knowledge of from personal experience or observation. In any case, we have no information apart from the biblical text. Thus, the descriptions of prophets in action in 1 and 2 Kings are an important source of data about Israelite prophets as well as about Israelite kings. The story of the prophet, the man of God, and Jeroboam in 1 Kings 13, as well as the story of Micaiah (1 Kgs 22), have implications for the question of 'true' prophecy versus 'false' prophecy.

Much more could be said on this whole topic, but it is beyond our purposes in the present volume. However, for more detail on the subject of prophets and prophecy, with extensive bibliography, see Grabbe 1995, Chapter 4.

The Books of Kings and Historiography

The historicity of Kings has also been much discussed, recently summarized by Avioz (2005, 2006). The books of Kings were always seen as having a religious or theological or moral connection, yet they were long read as a basis for ancient history. In the centuries before the decipherment of Mesopotamian cuneiform and Egyptian hieroglyphs, the Bible often provided the framework for the history of the Near East and even of Europe. As books that seemed to give a detailed history of Israel, 1 and 2 Kings were read off as straightforward history books. This does not mean that they were without problems of interpretation, but the other historical sources known at the time (meaning primarily the writings of Greek and Roman historians) all had their problems.

The biblical writings are no longer seen as the basis of world history, as they once were, but most of the standard histories of Israel used the biblical text as their main source. This might seem inevitable, since the text gives more detail than any other source, but it assumes a good deal of reliable historical information was available there. Where the history deviated the greatest from the biblical picture was primarily in the period before Saul, and this varied from history of Israel to history of Israel. But even those who argued the history only really began with David and Solomon (e.g. Soggin 1999) still followed the text heavily in 1 and 2 Kings.

The question is, what counts as 'history'? Some will accept the term 'history' to describe a writing that shows an interest in the past, an 'antiquarian interest', to employ the phrase used by Baruch Halpern (1988, 216). Others, such as myself, would argue that the term 'history' rightly applies only to narratives that arise from critical inquiry (Grabbe 2001). Let's examine why the biblical text could be called 'history' in a modern critical sense only if certain criteria were met.

The Question of Definitions
Unfortunately, much of the debate about the 'first historians' revolves around—or even depends upon—the particular definition one uses for 'history'. There is no doubt that the most influential recent work on the question is John Van Seters' *In Search of History* (1983). He draws heavily on Johan Huizinga's now classical statement, 'History is the intellectual form in which a civilization renders account to itself of its past'. Van Seters isolates the following characteristics of history writing:

1. A specific form of tradition in its own right.
2. Not primarily the accurate reporting of past events but also the reason for recalling the past and the significance given to past events.
3. Examination of the causes of present conditions and circumstances.
4. National or corporate in character. The reporting of the deeds of the king may be only biographical unless these are viewed as part of the national history. Toward the end of the book, he states that 'to communicate through this story of the people's past a sense of their identity…is the *sine qua non* of history writing' (Van Seters 1983, 359).
5. Part of the literary tradition and plays a significant role in the corporate tradition of the people (Van Seters 1983, 4-5).

Although Van Seters specifically draws on Huizinga's statement and claims that his criteria are in keeping with Huizinga's 'definition', it seems to me that his own formulation actually goes against Huizinga at various points. For one thing, Van Seters seems to see history writing as a single genre, whereas Huizinga is referring to history as a total enterprise. Huizinga also clearly includes writings as history that Van Seters would exclude:

> It comprises every form of historical record; that of the annalist, the writer of memoirs, the historical philosopher, and the scholarly researcher. It comprehends the smallest antiquarian monograph in the same sense as the vastest conception of world history. (Huizinga 1936, 10)

Huizinga's statement is not really a definition; it is not primarily an attempt to tell whether to categorize a particular work as history, but that is precisely what Van Seters is seeking. Contrary to Huizinga, Van Seters wants to exclude annalists as historians. He also wants to exclude descriptions of the king's deeds; indeed, he strangely excludes biography as a historical work, whereas most historians would include biography as a form of history writing. Especially problematic to me is that Van Seters wants to exclude anything that is not national or corporate in character. But few modern historians would see their work as national or corporate, nor do most modern historians of ancient history feel that they must of necessity examine the causes of present conditions and circumstances.

The problem with this definition and these characteristics is that they do not always characterize what contemporary historians do, and any definition that excludes the work of modern historians cannot be acceptable in the debate. Few historians in the modern academic world see themselves as furthering national goals, and most would argue that although their historical writing represents an interpretation, that interpretation is still based on certain methodological principles of critical argument, evidence, and falsifiable hypotheses.

Another example is Van Seters' statement that tradition does not become history until it deals with the people as a whole. Thus, a catalogue of the king's deeds is not history (Van Seters 1983, 2). Once again I find this rather difficult: by this criterion we would have to exclude Arrian's history of Alexander's conquests because it is by and large about Alexander. Any criterion which excluded a work like Arrian's or Caesar's *Gallic War* must be seen as absurd from the outset.

Thomas L. Thompson (1992a, 372-73; 1992b, 3:206-12) has produced a definition that is very much in keeping with modern sensibilities. According to Thompson,

> ...the ancient and particularly the classical Greek genre of historiography used the term in a much narrower, more restrictive sense. This more distinctive meaning has been maintained also in its present usage, namely, as a specific literary genre relating to critical descriptions and evaluations of past reality and events, in contrast to more fictional varieties of prose. (1992a, 372-73)

For Thompson, to call this 'historiography' and not 'history writing' is confusing but, in fact, his definition is really a definition of *critical* historical writing.

In order to answer the question of whether 1 and 2 Kings is an example of critical history writing, we need to compare it with historical writing elsewhere in the ancient world. Where did critical historical methodology develop and how does the Hebrew Bible match up to it? The place to go is to those long acknowledged by all to be pioneers in trying to write critical history: the ancient Greeks.

Development of Historical Writing among the Greeks

The development of historical writing among the Greeks is a good example to use because it is so well documented. This does not mean that examples of critical history writing cannot be found elsewhere in ancient times, but this gives us something that will serve our purposes. The real impetus for writing history arose out of the 'Ionian enlightenment', the same movement from which sprang the first philosophers and scientists (known as the 'pre-Socratics'). These early Greek philosophers who preceded Socrates, Plato, and Aristotle are often preserved only in fragments and not always easy to understand. Nevertheless, what is clear is they began to ask questions about the world, about nature, and about existence. From such thinkers we have an early form of the theory of atoms and the sun as the centre of the universe. It was here among the Greeks that we first have attested the important critical attitudes that led to scientific inquiry. The same attitudes were essential to the development of the true historical method.

Hecataeus of Miletus is one of the first historical writers about whom we know anything extensive, even if his work has not been preserved intact; however, we do have indications that he championed the principle so important to subsequent Greek historians, that of *autopsy* or seeing for yourself. Not having his work intact creates problems of interpretation, but some of his comments show a critical spirit of mind:

Hecataeus the Milesian speaks so: I write the things that follow as they seem
to me to be true. For the stories of the Greeks are both many and, as they
appear to me, ridiculous.

Aegyptus did not himself go to Argos, but his sons did—fifty of them in
Hesiod's story, but as I reckon not even twenty. [Translations from Derow
1994, 74]

Hecataeus shows the sceptical frame of mind required of all scientists and
critical scholars, including critical historians. He asks for evidence; he is
not afraid to label popular belief as incredible.

Herodotus. Even with all the excavations and new finds, Herodotus
remains the 'father of history'. In his writing we can see the historian at
work and are able to make explicit deductions about the process of critical
historiography. Herodotus contains all sorts of material, to the point that
some would see him as more of a travel writer than a historian. But a
number of points arise from study of his work, some explicit and some
implicit (for further on Herodotus as a historian, see Grabbe 2015):
    1. Herodotus accepts reports of events and forms of causation that
would not be entertained by modern historians. Divine causation is taken
for granted. On the other hand, we should not be too patronizing about this:
acceptance of divine causation is not all that different from metaphysical
causes that some modern historians have proposed with great seriousness.
Some modern historians have seen such intangible drivers of history as an
organistic development of nations (birth, youth, maturity, senility, death
[Spengler 1926–28]).
    2. Herodotus himself shows a critical spirit in a number of explicit
instances. For example, he critiques the standard story of the Trojan
war and gives reasons why another version is more likely to be correct
(2.118-20). He also questions stories that he has heard but records them
nevertheless, such as the position of the sun in the circumnavigation of
Africa (4.42). In this he does not differ in kind from a modern historian
who collects data and then attempts to evaluate it critically. The fact that
Herodotus happened to have been wrong about the incident of the sun is
irrelevant; after all, complete accuracy in judgment is also hardly a trait
of modern historical study.
    3. We have a fair amount of indirect evidence that Herodotus used
good sources for important aspects of his history. His account of Darius
I's taking of the throne is consonant with and complementary to the information we have from Darius's own inscription at Behistun (3.61-87; see

especially Balcer 1987). Although he does not name his informants in this particular case, he has evidently consulted members of the Persian aristocracy. The ability to choose and interrogate good sources is part of the critical historical work.

Thucydides. Herodotus was quickly followed by Thucydides whose methodological innovations still meet the standards of modern historical research (cf. Hornblower 1987). Thucydides tells us about some of the criteria he applied in his work (1.20-22, translations from Warner 1954, 46-48):

> In investigating past history, and in forming the conclusions which I have formed, it must be admitted that one cannot rely on every detail which has come down to us by way of tradition. People are inclined to accept all stories of ancient times in an uncritical way—even when these stories concern their own native countries... (1.20.1)

> And with regard to my factual reporting of the events of the war I have made it a principle not write down the first story that came my way, and not even to be guided by my own general impressions; either I was present myself at the events which I have described or else I heard of them from eye-witnesses whose reports I have checked with as much thoroughness as possible. Not that even so the truth was easy to discover: different eye-witnesses give different accounts of the same events, speaking out of partiality for one side or the other or else from imperfect memories. And it may well be that my history will seem less easy to read because of the absence in it of a romantic element. (1.22.2-4)

Some of the principles used by Thucydides include the following (though some of these are already to be found among his predecessors):

1. The traditions about the early history of Greece untrustworthy and to be given no credence.
2. The interrogation of eye witnesses and the collection of a variety of eye witness and other accounts. Although Thucydides unfortunately tells only of the account that he finds most trustworthy, from all we can tell he does appear to have followed his own rule.
3. A critical judgment made on the various accounts to select the one that appears to be most credible according to common-sense criteria.
4. The establishment of a chronological framework which dates all events to within six months.

These are important rules and are still applied in some form or other by most modern historians. Thucydides was by common consent the pinnacle of history writers in antiquity, and his successors did not rise to quite the same heights. Xenophon, who continued his history of the Peloponnesian War, was not of the same calibre. Yet Xenophon wrote an important account (the *Anabasis*) of his own adventures in Persia during the 401 BCE attempt to take the throne by Cyrus the Younger. On the other hand, most modern scholars consider the *Cyropaedia*, which ostensibly gives a life of Cyrus the founder of the Persian empire, as unreliable on the whole and to be used only cautiously and critically for information about Persian history (e.g., J. Tatum 1989). However, the anonymous writer known as the Oxyrhynchus Historian is thought to give a quite accurate portrayal of a few years of the Peloponnesian War; unfortunately, the author of this work is unidentified, and the principles on which it was written have yet to be determined (cf. Bruce 1967).

Polybius. Probably the second place in the ranks of ancient historians is held by Polybius. He was an important historian who wrote not only about contemporary events that he witnessed himself but also about Roman history from the First Punic War, more than a century before his own time. Perhaps more than any other ancient historian Polybius discusses the principles guiding him in the writing of his history. Some of the points he makes are the following:

1. The historian cannot show favouritism. He points out that one expects to favour one's friends and country, but

> he who assumes the character of a historian must ignore everything of the sort, and often, if their actions demand this, speak good of his enemies and honour them with the highest praises while criticizing and even reproaching roundly his closest friends, should the errors of their conduct impose this duty on him. (1.14, translation from Paton 1922–27)

2. It is the duty of the historian not just to narrate or assemble 'facts' but to explain the cause (*aitia*) of and connections between events. The historian must explain the 'how, why, and whence' (*pōs, dia ti, pothen*) or the 'when, how, and for what reason' (*pote, pōs, di' has aitias*) with regard to events (3.7; 4.28.4).
3. Although it had become conventional from Thucydides on to include speeches in historical works, many of his successors ignored his principles and concentrated on exercising rhetorical skills. Polybius insists that speeches must reflect what was actually said: 'nor is it the

proper part of a historian to practise on his readers and make a display of his ability to them, but rather to find out by the most diligent inquiry and report to them what was actually said' (36.1.7).

4. He emphasizes his own efforts to travel and question witnesses (3.57-59; 12.25g-25i; 12.26d-28a). Polybius is scathing of the 'arm-chair historians' (entire book 12).

Whether the Greek historians rose to the standards expected for modern historians can be discussed for particular writers, but it was a common-place expectation that the historian's first concern was faithfulness to the data and accuracy in presenting them, even if it was generally anticipated that he would also write an interesting and elevating account. For most ancient readers the real essence of history was its truth. This view was voiced by 'Antonius' in Cicero's dialogue in *De Oratore* (2.15.62):

> For who does not know history's first law to be that an author must not dare to tell anything but the truth? And its second that he must make bold to tell the whole truth? That there must be no suggestion of partiality anywhere in his writings? Nor of malice?

This is not to suggest that all Greek 'historians' from Herodotus on are examples of critical historians. On the contrary, many of them fall well short of even minimum standards as exemplified in Herodotus and Thucydides. Perhaps the nadir to Thucydides's zenith is Ctesias of Cnidus (the main study remains König 1972). Ctesias wrote about the same time as Xenophon and is thus a successor of the great historians. After being captured by the Persians and serving for 17 years as the personal physician of Artaxerxes II, he should have been in a good position to report on many aspects of the Persian court and Persian history at first hand. Instead, he compiled a farrago of legends, inventions, and gossip that was already denounced in antiquity (e.g., by Plutarch, *Artaxerxes* 1.4).

To summarize, the quality of historical writing in Greco-Roman antiquity varied enormously (though this statement would apply equally to today), and there was an inevitable division between theory and practice. Yet the best historical work rose to modern standards, including such writers as Thucydides and Polybius and even other writers such as Arrian on Alexander. Most scholars of classical historiography would be in no doubt that critical historiography had developed in the Greco-Roman historical tradition. (For further on this question, see Grabbe 2001.)

Summary with Regard to History
I would like to summarize this section with the following observations:

1. A variety of valid definitions can be advanced, depending on the
    perspective from which one approaches the subject. I would simply
    argue that whatever definition is used, it must not exclude any of
    the writers of antiquity called 'historians' by common consent, and
    it certainly must not exclude the work of modern historians.
2. The question of definition is important because one's conclusions
    can often be anticipated in the definition one uses of 'history' or
    'history writing'. Some of the present debate unfortunately turns
    on definition.
3. For our purposes, we are asking about *critical* historical writing.
    Thompson's definition above seems to approximate what I have
    in mind. By 'critical historical writing' I do not mean a particular
    'positivistic' form of writing. I have reference to the term 'critical'
    as used in a wide sense in modern scholarship to refer to an attitude
    or approach which does not take things at face value but shows a
    certain scepticism, asks questions about epistemology and rational
    explanation, is most concerned about human causation, and wants
    to test the evidence. My definition does not rule out approaches
    which attempt to apply a grand scheme to history (e.g., an evolu-
    tionary model), for this has been characteristic of a number of
    modern historians (e.g., Marxist interpretation).

The question is, do 1 and 2 Kings meet the criteria just enumerated?
Chapters 3–5 discuss this question.

Some Major Commentaries on 1 and 2 Kings

I wish to finish this chapter by listing and discussing briefly some of the
major commentaries on 1 and 2 Kings. Commentaries take a variety of
approaches and are written for a variety of audiences. The first to consider
is a slightly older commentary by James A. Montgomery, *A Critical and
Exegetical Commentary on the Books of Kings*. This was in the famous
commentary series, the International Critical Commentary, that often
concentrated on textual and historical matters and questions in critical
scholarship. The original series began in the late 1800s, but the Kings
commentary was one of the last ones published in the original series; it was
completed by H.S. Gehman and came out in 1951, after Montgomery's

death. The series has been revived and new volumes are coming out to fill in the gaps, though whether Kings will be redone is not yet clear. (One should really know Hebrew to appreciate this series.) A Dutch series of commentaries being translated into English as the Historical Commentary on the Old Testament has some of the same objectives as the International Critical Commentary. It aims to give attention to the history of the biblical tradition in all its stages, both within and outside the Hebrew canon, and is historically critically oriented. The first volume available (of several planned) on Kings is Martin I. Muller, *1 Kings, Volume 1: 1 Kings 1–11* (1998), a substantial and up-to-date treatment of the text.

The Anchor Bible has two volumes on Kings: Mordechai Cogan, *I Kings: A New Translation with Introduction and Commentary* (2001) and Mordechai Cogan and Hayim Tadmor, *II Kings: A New Translation with Introduction and Commentary* (1988). These are especially valuable for the historical and archaeological context of the biblical text, both the authors being specialists in Akkadian (Assyrian) literature. Volkmar Fritz, *1 & 2 Kings: A Continental Commentary* (2003) is a translation of two volumes in the Zürcher Bibelkommentar series. In keeping with the German commentary aims, the treatment is somewhat compressed, with only minimal treatment of composition and textual growth. Its value is primarily in archaeology and comparison with other ancient Near Eastern texts to illuminate the historical and literary context of the biblical tradition.

John Gray, *I and II Kings* (2d ed., 1970) and the more recent commentary by Marvin A. Sweeney, *I & II Kings: A Commentary* (2007) are both in the Old Testament Library. This series seeks to present the significant historical, linguistic, literary, and theological aspects of the text in a highly readable format. Jerome T. Walsh, *1 Kings* (1996), and Robert L. Cohn, *2 Kings* (2000), contribute to the Berit Olam commentary series, which aims to use the modern method of literary criticism; that is, the authors approach the books of the Hebrew Bible as literary works. In their analysis of the text, they apply our knowledge of the techniques used by the ancient writers to tell stories and write poems (the subtitle of the series is Studies in Hebrew Narrative and Poetry), as well as the strategies that modern readers can use to understand them. Walter Brueggemann, *1 and 2 Kings* (2000) in the Smyth & Helwys Bible Commentary series, is not primarily a verse-by-verse commentary but focuses on the meaning of the text for today. Brueggemann is an inimitable commentator whom many find refreshing (though some object to his attacks on certain modern institutions).

Simon DeVries, *1 Kings* (1985) and T.R. Hobbs, *2 Kings* (1986) both
write in the Word Bible Commentary. This series tends to be on the
conservative side but often engages with standard scholarship on historical and critical matters (e.g., both authors accept that 1 and 2 Kings is
a Deuteronomistic work [discussed further in Chapter 2 of the present
volume]). Gwilym H. Jones, *1 and 2 Kings* (1984) writes in the New
Century Bible that attempts to reach a wider audience. Yet the author is
a well-known critical scholar and provides considerable historical and
theological insight. Iain W. Provan, *1 and 2 Kings* (1995), writes in the
New International Bible Commentary series, with a literary and historical analysis from the point of view of conservative evangelical theology.
Burke O. Long gives primarily a form critical analysis of the text: *1 Kings,
with an Introduction to Historical Literature* (1984) and *2 Kings* (1991).
His studies will be considered in Chapter 2 and subsequent chapters of
the present volume.

Several volumes already mentioned have been translated from other
languages into English. Many of the commentaries in German are now
getting quite old and will not be listed here. But for those who read
German, a couple of commentaries can be mentioned. The well-known
German Old Testament scholar and historian Martin Noth (who will be
mentioned in Chapter 2 and subsequent chapters) began a commentary,
1 und 2 Könige, in the series Biblischer Kommentar (which he founded).
He covered only the first 16 chapters with verse-by-verse commentary,
which is very valuable, but unfortunately he had not written an introduction to the books when he died in 1968. The task is being taken forward by
Winfried Thiel, who has so far published comments on 1 Kgs 17.1–21.29.
This series is a leading critical commentary series in German, represent-
ing the current state of research. Ernst Würthwein, *Die Bücher der Könige*
(1977–84) contributes to another series, the Alt Testament Deutsch. This
also attempts to present up-to-date scholarship, in the following standard
format: introduction, literature, accurate translation, analysis and interpretation of text. Many of its volumes have been translated into English for
the series Old Testament Library. (One could also mention the Zürcher
Bibelkommentar, which was already named above, since two of its
volumes by Volkmar Fritz were translated into English.)

The list here is by no means exhaustive, but the volumes mentioned
here should provide considerable food for thought for readers of the
present volume. Full bibliographical details for each item can be found in
the bibliography at the end of this book.

Chapter 2

THE BOOKS OF KINGS
AND 'THE DEUTERONOMISTIC HISTORY':
FORM AND SOURCE CRITICISM

In this chapter we shall consider the composition and development of 1 and 2 Kings, as well as some of the main literary genres found in it. These will serve as a basis for making historical judgments in subsequent chapters.

The Deuteronomistic History

For about three quarters of a century now, the books of Kings have become widely accepted as part of the 'Deuteronomistic history' (DH; the author/editor is often called the 'Deuteronomistic historian' or DtrH). This concept was developed by Martin Noth and was laid out in his 1943 monograph (ET 1981). Noth's original thesis argued that a 'Deuteronomistic school' (which had developed among the Deuteronomists who had originated the book of Deuteronomy) created a unified composition made up of the books of Deuteronomy to 2 Kings in the Hebrew Bible. According to this theory, Joshua to 2 Kings were compiled and edited from pre-existent source material along with the contribution of the Deuteronomistic editor. The core of the book of Deuteronomy was placed at the beginning of this document to introduce it, and Deuteronomy 1–4 (not originally a part of the book of Deuteronomy) was written to introduce the entire DH. The book itself was composed/compiled during the exile, about 560 BCE. The reason was to provide a theological explanation for the disaster that came on Judah.

This thesis has been widely accepted in scholarship over the decades in a general way (see especially Römer and De Pury 2000 for a summary of Noth's original thesis and subsequent developments). During this time, however, the concept of a DH has gone through a variety of developments and assessments. For some the DH is simply a collection of the books from

Joshua to 2 Kings, perhaps even a loose collection of books. This was not Martin Noth's original concept, nor is it the perspective of a number of modern critics, though Noth's thesis has also been adapted, revised, and even rejected. Two major alternatives have developed in recent years (Römer and De Pury 2000, 62-74). One is that of the so-called 'Göttingen School', initiated primarily by Rudolph Smend. In many ways, it is close to the original hypothesis of Noth. According to this scheme, an original Deuteronomistic historian (DtrH) created the original work about 580 BCE. This was revised by a redactor whose main concern was with the law, known as the Nomistic editor (DtrN), about 560 BCE. Some of Smend's students suggested a third level of editing, the insertion of prophetic judgments and their fulfilment, known as the Prophetic Deuteronomist (DtrP), dated sometime between the DtrH and the DtrN. Thus, although in certain ways parallel to Noth, with an initial Deuteronomistic compilation, the Smend model proposes that this first level was then twice redacted, primarily in the exilic period. A considerable number of scholars, especially in Germany, have accepted the basic thesis, though it is not unusual for the details to be disputed.

The other main alternative is the thesis of a 'double redaction', credited primarily to Frank Cross and widely accepted in the English-speaking world (an important exposition is given in Nelson 1981). It proposes that the first stage was a composition at the time of Josiah's reforms, which was an optimistic writing that celebrated the achievements of the Davidic dynasty. After the disaster of the fall of Jerusalem, this edition was worked over by an exilic redactor who expressed the shock and disappointment experienced and assigned the destruction of the kingdom of Judah to theological causes, primarily disobedience of Yhwh and his prophets. Thus, two layers are presupposed, each with its own outlook and theology.

To summarize, the composition of the DH continues to be debated (Römer 2005; Lipschits 2005, 272-304; O'Brien 1989; Campbell and O'Brien 2000). Most specialists choose between an ascription to a single composition in the sixth century (with minor edits at a later time), a three-fold composition in the sixth century (with perhaps some continuing editing through the Persian period), or a two-fold composition, the first edition in the late seventh century and the second in the exilic period. In each case, the compiler(s) would have used a variety of traditions, as well as making their own edits and additions. Yet there have also been doubts about the existence of the DH as a unified document (e.g. Knauf 2000).

The Main Genres of 1 and 2 Kings

Regardless of which theory is followed about the broader context of 1 and 2 Kings—or even if you follow no particular theory—it is clear that the two books contain a number of literary genres, some which are quite frequent in the books. These served as the sources of the writer of 1 and 2 Kings or were in some cases the literary forms in which he expressed himself. These are laid out by Burke O. Long in the main form critical commentary on the books of Kings (Long 1984, 4-8):

List. This gave a list of items, sometimes without any particular principle of order, but in some lists there is a clear basis for the order of the things listed. In some cases, lists contained historical information, whether of events, names of persons, names of places, or the like. *Genealogy* is a type of list that might contain historical data. Another is the *King List* (though king lists as such are not found in 1 and 2 Kings). Here and there in the biblical text are lists of rulers (Gen. 36.31-39), royal officials (1 Kgs 4.2-19), items taken as booty (Num. 31.32-40), and the like.

Report. This is defined as 'a brief, self-contained narrative, usually in third-person style, about a single event or situation in the past' (Long 1984, 5). This genre is of particular interest because *Annals* are just a series of scribal reports. These can lead to an edited selection of events arranged and dated in chronological order, called a *Chronicle*. It has been argued that a chronicle or set of chronicles were among the sources used by the author of Kings, and this will be discussed at greater length in the next section. (Just to be clear, this is not the biblical books of Chronicles—see below, pp. 21-22.)

Official Report. It will perhaps be surprising that the 'Report' is distinguished from the 'Official Report' (Long 1984, 5, 253-54). The latter is sent by an authorized person by messenger to an authorized recipient. It normally has the following constituent parts: (1) commissioning of a messenger, (2) the going forth and reception of the messenger, (3) the message which is quoted directly, (4) the reaction of the recipient. Examples of official reports are found in 1 Kgs 20.2-3, 5-6, 32.

Legend. This is a narrative or story that is 'concerned primarily with the wondrous, miraculous, and exemplary' (Long 1984, 252). Although the legend may have the object of entertainment, its main concern is edification. It may enhance respect or devotion for a holy place or holy person, or it may serve as a medium of instruction by providing models of morality or piety. Unlike 'History' or the 'Historical Story' (see below), it has no obligation to narrate actual events, though it may of course relate to or be based in part on real happenings. Because it is primarily a genre arising from folk tradition, it develops in its own way as oral literature of the community, though in the form we have it, it might have been shaped in this final form by a literary writer.

In 1 and 2 Kings we have a number of *Prophetic Legends*, of which there are many in the biblical text. These usually present the prophet in question as a model of piety, virtue, and obedience, but they often show him performing miraculous acts, such as healing or even raising the dead (with God's help, naturally). The main examples in 1 and 2 Kings are the Elijah and Elisha legends (see Chapter 4, pp. 56-57 below).

Königsnovelle (or 'Royal Novella', also called a *Royal Narrative*). This was first identified in Egyptian texts that showed the Pharaoh as a model of sagacity, strength, leadership, and devotion to the gods. However, if we look more widely we can see kings from other areas who fit this description. For a more lengthy discussion of this genre see below (pp. 31-33).

Historical Story. This is a narrative concerned to recount a particular event but is distinguished from a report by its greater literary sophistication. There may be dramatic elements or other characteristics associated with fiction, but it differs from legend, tale, and fiction in general by its purpose, which is to recount events as they were thought to have happened. The main problem we have with this genre is determining whether a narrative has such a historical purpose, since many of the stories that might be historical also lend themselves to instruction, entertainment, or edification, which is not supposed to be the chief aim of a historical story. This applies to supposed examples of the historical story in 1 Kings (e.g. 12.1-20; 20.1-43; 22.1-37).

History. This is defined as 'an extensive, continuous, written composition made up of various materials, originally oral and/or written, and devoted to a particular subject or historical period' (Long 1984, 7). The writer may make use of elements that an author of fiction might also employ. The *Biography* and the *Memoir* form a special type of history. We have no examples of biography as such in the Hebrew Bible, though Nehemiah contains an example of a memoir. But as with the 'History Story', the question of whether there is actually an example of a narrative that we can label as 'history' is a question that cannot be answered by fiat or definition: we have to explore the characteristics of the narrative and ask whether it is genuinely history according to the criteria of a modern historian. This was the question we asked at the end of Chapter 1, and it is the question that we shall take up in more detail in Chapters 3–5.

The Use of Court Chronicles as a Source of the Deuteronomistic History

It was long ago suggested that an important source for the author of 1 and 2 Kings was an official court or royal chronicle. Menahem Haran traces the idea back at least to the nineteenth century (1999, 157 n. 2). When Noth wrote his seminal essay, he made it clear that the author of the DH had acted in many ways as a compiler, for he often incorporated material with little or no editing, with his editorial work frequently confined to linking material or to decisions about where to place the traditions at his disposal. Noth accepted that official chronicles were among the DtrH's sources (Noth 1943, 114-20; 1981, 63-68), an idea that was by no means new: indeed, he referred to it as 'generally known' that the DtrH based much of the books of Kings on the *Chronicle of the Kings of Israel* (henceforth referred to as *CKI*) and the *Chronicle of the Kings of Judah* (*CKJ*: Noth 1943, 114-15; 1981, 63). In Noth's view these 'chronicles' (*Tagebücher*) provided only the framework for the history, and other sorts of material (e.g. prophetic legends) were used to fill up the narrative. His main point was that the Deuteronomist used a variety of sources in creating the Deuteronomistic History, and he did not attempt to delineate the two chronicles further.

Please note that we are speaking of *extra-biblical chronicles*, not the biblical books of Chronicles (which are always capitalized). A brief survey of commentaries shows that the *Chronicle of the Kings of Israel* (*CKI*) and the *Chronicle of the Kings of Judah* (*CKJ*) or something similar are often assumed to be important sources for the DH. In 1953, published in 1956, Alfred Jepsen developed a theory about the redaction of 1 and 2 Kings built on several sources and redactors, including a 'synchronistic chronicle' (*synchronistische Chronik*) and a set of 'annals' (*Annalenwerk*). Several others also analyzed the formulae, with the objective of getting at the redactional layers of the DH (see further Grabbe 2006); however, I shall mention here only Nadav Na'aman who has written a good deal on the question of the sources used by the DtrH (1997, 1999, 2003, 2005a), and Menahem Haran (1999) who has looked at the specific question of the *CKI* and *CKJ*. There are a number of reasons for postulating a native chronicle as a major source:

1. Official chronicles of various sorts, connected to the royal court, are widely known from the ancient Near East.
2. We appear to have a reference to Israelite and Judahite chronicles in DH itself (e.g. 1 Kgs 14.19-20, 29-31; 15.7-8, 23-24, 27-31; 16.5-6, 10-14, 18-20, 27-28). Can we take this at face value, or could the author simply be inventing sources to give plausibility to his account? The latter is possible, though the direct citation of sources is an obsession of modern historians and not one widespread in ancient historiographic works. Considering the extensive evidence for such chronicles in the ancient Near East, it seems unlikely that the author was inventing fictitious sources.
3. A number of stereotyped formulae that introduce and summarize the reigns of different kings might suggest borrowing from a source. For further on this, see below.
4. Some reliable historical data for the reigns of Israelite and Judahite kings during the period of the 'Divided Monarchy' have been demonstrated (e.g. the names, order, and approximate time frame of the kings). There is no denying the actual names of Israelite and Judahite kings as found in the Assyrian records. If the DH was compiled at a late date, such as the exilic period or even the time of Josiah, where did the compiler obtain such information? Historical data are most likely to have come from a written source, but the sort of source that would contain that type of data consistently is a chronicle.

Accepting that there is evidence for the use of a chronicle or chronicles as an important source by the DtrH, and building on previous studies, I have attempted to characterize that source. The following paragraphs summarize some of the main points in my study that argues the question (Grabbe 2006), which should be consulted for further references and a more complete argument.

The text refers to both the *CKI* and the *CKJ*, and it has usually been assumed that the author used two sources, which he synchronized himself. Briefly, I have proposed that it is not necessary to assume two chronicles since all the chronicle data in 1 and 2 Kings could have come from a single chronicle, the *Chronicle of the Kings of Judah*. The synchronic data about the kings of Israel would also have been present in the *CKJ*. My thesis is that a single chronicle—*CKJ*—was used by the author/compiler of the DH for the framework of his history, for the 'Divided Monarchy'. This chronicle gave brief but factual information on each king of Judah but also recorded the accession and deaths of the neighbouring kingdom of Israel. Other (often legendary or semi-legendary) material was used by the DtrH to fill out the narrative, but much of the reliable data—the data confirmed by other ancient Near Eastern sources—was taken from the *CKJ*. This chronicle had several characteristics:

- Basic accession data but also including the name of the king's mother.
- Data on its main neighbour and rival, the Kingdom of Israel, including the synchronic data.
- Brief notes on major events in the king's reign. These were not necessarily stereotyped but could include a wide variety of data relating to the military, politics, building activities, personal matters relating to the king (e.g. major illnesses), and the cult. This was not according to a rigid formula.

When we start to ask what the *CKJ* might have looked like, it seems to me that we have a number of indications in the biblical text itself. First, we notice the recurrence of three formulae. One of these is about the accession of the king and one is about the death of the king, which are the formulae of interest here. A third formula (often studied) is a theological evaluation of the king's reign and is certainly the contribution of the DtrH and will not be further discussed. No chronicle is likely to have included a theological judgment of the king's rule, especially since these evaluations found throughout the DH are mostly negative. No example of such evaluations is found in any of the other chronicles known from the ancient Near East, but this precisely fits the aim of the Deuteronomistic compiler who is composing a theological account of the history of Israel and Judah. A typical example concerns the reign of Abijam of Judah (1 Kgs 15.1-8 NRSV):

> *¹Now in the eighteenth year of King Jeroboam son of Nebat, Abijam began to reign over Judah. ²He reigned for three years in Jerusalem. His mother's name was Maacah daughter of Abishalom.* ³He committed all the sins that his father did before him; his heart was not true to the LORD his God, like the heart of his father David. ⁴Nevertheless for David's sake the LORD his God gave him a lamp in Jerusalem, setting up his son after him, and establishing Jerusalem; ⁵because David did what was right in the sight of the LORD, and did not turn aside from anything that he commanded him all the days of his life, except in the matter of Uriah the Hittite. *⁶The war begun between Rehoboam and Jeroboam continued all the days of his life.* ⁷The rest of the acts of Abijam, and all that he did, are they not written in the Book of the Annals of the Kings of Judah? *There was war between Abijam and Jeroboam.* ⁸Abijam slept with his ancestors, and they buried him in the city of David. Then his son Asa succeeded him.

This shows two formulae, one about the accession of the king (marked with a dashed underline) and one about the death of the king (marked with a dashed underline). The information that might have been borrowed from the *CKJ* is given in italics. The text in regular Roman type is the contribution of the DtrH, either his own statement or theological judgment or material from other sources. It is unlikely that both the italicized statement in v. 6 and that at the end of v. 7 are quotations from *CKJ*, but the chronicle must have had a statement on the war. It illustrates that the author adapted material from the *CKJ* and did not always just quote it verbatim. Verses 3-5 are clearly the contribution of the Deuteronomistic editor.

An important conclusion immediately manifests itself: *All of the real information in this passage could have come from a chronicle*. In addition to the information in vv. 1-2, a chronicle entry might well have mentioned that Abijam waged war against Jeroboam all his reign (vv. 6-7). The statements in vv. 3-5 are part of the Deuteronomistic repertoire (theological pronouncements, in this case) but do not constitute 'information', in the sense of telling us something about the king's reign.

Now let us consider the continuation of the passage, the reign of Asa of Judah (1 Kgs 15.9-24):

[9]In the twentieth year of King Jeroboam of Israel, Asa began to reign over Judah; [10]he reigned forty-one years in Jerusalem. His mother's name was Maacah daughter of Abishalom. [11]Asa did what was right in the sight of the LORD, as his father David had done. [12]He put away the male temple prostitutes out of the land, and removed all the idols that his ancestors had made. [13]*He also removed his mother Maacah from being queen mother*, because she had made an abominable image for Asherah; Asa cut down her image and burned it at the Wadi Kidron. [14]But the high places were not taken away. Nevertheless the heart of Asa was true to the LORD all his days. [15]He brought into the house of the LORD the votive gifts of his father and his own votive gifts—silver, gold, and utensils. [16]*There was war between Asa and King Baasha of Israel all their days. [17]King Baasha of Israel went up against Judah, and built Ramah*, to prevent anyone from going out or coming in to King Asa of Judah. [18]Then Asa took all the silver and the gold that were left in the treasures of the house of the LORD and the treasures of the king's house, and gave them into the hands of his servants. *King Asa sent* them *to King Ben-hadad son of Tabrimmon son of Hezion of Aram, who resided in Damascus, saying,*

[19]'Let there be an alliance between me and you, like that between my father and your father: I am sending you a present of silver and gold; go, break your alliance with King Baasha of Israel, so that he may withdraw from me'.

[20]*Ben-hadad* listened to King Asa, and sent the commanders of his armies against the cities of Israel. He *conquered Ijon, Dan, Abel-beth-maacah, and all Chinneroth, with all the land of Naphtali.* [21]*When Baasha heard of it, he stopped building Ramah and lived in Tirzah.* [22]Then King Asa made a proclamation to all Judah, none was exempt: they carried away the stones of Ramah and its timber, with which Baasha had been building; with them King Asa built Geba of Benjamin and Mizpah. [23]Now the rest of all the acts of Asa, all his power, all that he did, and the cities that he built, are they not written in the Book of the Annals of the Kings of Judah? *But in his old age he was diseased in his feet.* [24]Then Asa slept with his ancestors, and was buried with his ancestors in the city of his father David; his son Jehoshaphat succeeded him.

This example is similar to the one on Abijam's reign, with the same basic accession and death formulae. But it is also longer, with more information, especially with regard to the cult and to the involvement of the king of Damascus. Did the compiler have other sources for the reign of Asa? Possibly, but it would not be necessary, since he could have taken everything here from a chronicle entry, apart from his own contribution from the stock Deuteronomistic repertoire. A suggestion of what the *CKJ* might have contained is indicated by the italicized text, though this can be no more than a guess based on what is found in other chronicles. It is not clear how much of the cultic activity described in vv. 12-14 might have been in the *CKJ*, though some of the data might have been. Some of the content of v. 15 was probably in the chronicle, as was some of vv. 17-21, but it would have been bare factual statements: the explanatory material is probably the contribution of the DH editor. The contents of v. 22 might also have been in the chronicle.

Thus, these two formulae emerge that might have been a part of the original chronicle and not just a stereotyped expression of the Deuteronomist. The first is an *accession formula*:

a. In the nth year of king PN of Israel/Judah, PN son of PN became king.
[b. He was n years old when he became king.]
c. And he reigned n years in Jerusalem/Samaria.
[d. His mother's name was PN.]

This formula takes two slightly different forms, depending on whether it refers to a king of Israel or a king of Judah. Points *b* and *d* are not found for Israelite kings, but their (mostly) consistent presence with Judahite kings indicates that they were likely to have been included in the chronicle entry for each Judahite king. It is important to note that this formula is not rigid and was adapted to take care of unusual events such as assassination or usurpation.

The second formula relates to the end of the ruler's reign, and can perhaps be called the *death* or *closing formula*:

e.   And the rest of the deeds of PN and all that he did—are they not written in the Book of the Matters of Days of the King of Israel/ Judah (a literal rendering of the Hebrew name)?

[f.   Reference to a specific deed (or occasionally deeds) of the king.]

g.   PN slept with his fathers and was buried in the GN.

h.   His son PN became king in his place.

Since no chronicle entry would contain a cross reference to itself, point *e* did not come from *CKJ*. Point *g* could be from the chronicle but could also be the DtrH's own invention. Point *h* repeats information in the accession formula and thus is probably not from the chronicle. Point *f* does not always occur (which is why it is in brackets), and sometimes it is embedded in the middle of point *e*. The information in it could well have come from a chronicle but probably not from a fixed formula.

When we examine these two formulae, it becomes clear that the opening formula is similar to chronicle entries in other ancient Near Eastern chronicles. Although no other chronicle mentions the name of the king's mother, this could be a cultural practice unique to Judah. Its consistent presence for Judahite kings but absence for Israelite kings suggests this. This opening formula seems to contain certain sorts of information that is conventionally found in official chronicles. Thus, there is a good possibility that the opening formula was taken from the *CKJ*. It might have been adapted but could in many cases be verbatim: since this is essential information for the DtrH's narrative, why not just copy from the chronicle? The closing formula is more difficult. As noted above, element *e* is unlikely to have come from any chronicle, but it is conceivable that a chronicle might regularly have a statement that a king 'slept with his fathers and his son reigned after him'; however, it is also possible that this is a DtrH invention, since it generally tells us nothing new. What does seem clear is that the opening formula—but not the closing—is likely to be a direct borrowing from the *CKJ*. A partial borrowing or an adaptation from a chronicle formula for the closing formula is possible, but it could just as well be an invention of the DtrH.

Is the use of only one chronicle as a source sufficient to explain this type of material in the DH? It is often assumed that the author made use of two sources, the *CKI* and the *CKJ*. Statements that synchronized the reigns of Israelite kings with the Judaean line have often been ascribed to the editor who supposedly combined two sets of annals. Yet, as Haran (1999, 158-59) asked, how would the author come into possession of two such chronicles? Na'aman has recently argued that the temple library was available to the compiler (2005a, 108). This would be reasonable if a version of DH was composed in the time of Josiah (as Na'aman and others have argued); however, this is less likely if the book is entirely an exilic composition, as is still widely accepted in German-speaking scholarship. But would even the temple library have had a copy of the *CKI*? It seems unlikely, and Haran's argument that the author would not have had two (or three, if we count the *Chronicle of the Acts of Solomon*) chronicles in front of him has force.

However, the ubiquitous thesis that a chronicle from the Northern Kingdom was available to the author is unnecessary, because we have examples of Mesopotamian chronicles that include information on the accession to the throne of kings in neighbouring regions (see Glassner 2004). The *Synchronistic Chronicle* has been mentioned along these lines, but it is not the best example of what we find in 1 and 2 Kings. There are other chronicles that have such data, however, and are closer to the format in 1 and 2 Kings, of which some excerpts were given. They provide excellent comparative evidence of how a single chronicle might well include accession data from neighbouring countries. A good example is Glassner's Chronicle 16, *From Nabonassar to Šamaš-Šuma-Ukīn* (Glassner 2004, 193-203; Chronicle 1 in Grayson 1975).

When we compare this format of chronicle from Mesopotamia to 1 and 2 Kings, a number of points are suggested for the postulated *CKJ*. Here are some of the features that the *CKJ* was likely to have possessed:

- It would be fairly concise, devoting only a paragraph to each king. Even if individual years were sometimes recorded, these would have been very short.
- The basic data included for each king would be the time of taking his throne, his father, his mother, and the length of his reign. In addition, some of the main events of his reign would be included (if there were any): battles, invasions, revolts, building projects, other significant events. Although stereotyped language might be used in describing these, the writer was ready to be flexible in the case of unusual events: the formula is not used rigidly.

- The synchronism of the reigns of the Israelite and Judahite kings (for the period up to 720 BCE) would also be part of this single chronicle. It would make sense if the compiler of a Judahite chronicle included information for its nearest (and stronger) neighbour.
- However, moral or religious judgment about the king would *not* be contained in the chronicle. Such information is a contribution of the DH editor/compiler.

Summary and Conclusion

If we look carefully at the material stretching from 1 Kings 16 to 2 Kings 17, we see few passages of any length that seem to be staightforward historical narratives. On the contrary, the whole section is dominated by prophetic stories or theological interests. For example, an entire chapter is devoted to the reign of Joash of Judah (2 Kgs 12), yet most of the space concerns how money was collected for the repair of the house of Yhwh. There is little from 1 Kings 17 to 2 Kings 9 that does not relate to Elijah and Elisha. Much of this long section of 15 chapters is a series of prophetic stories and anecdotes. Some of these relate to national events, but a good deal is purely focused on the doings of the prophets.

We have one new development, however, which is very important for the question of historicity. Beginning with the narrative of the 'divided monarchy' the DtrH seems to make use of a new source: a *Chronicle of the Kings of Judah* (Grabbe 2006). Considering the widespread evidence for such chronicles in the ancient Near East, it seems unlikely that the author was inventing fictitious sources. The *Chronicle of the Kings of Judah* seems to have provided the framework for the 'Divided Monarchy', but it was supplemented by much other material. The data that might have come from a chronicle are not extensive and could be explained as coming from a fairly concise chronicle such as we find in Mesopotamia.

As will be seen, some of the other sources may sometimes have contained reliable historical data, but most of the data in the text confirmed by external data as trustworthy could have come from such a chronicle. This means that the bulk of the DtrH's text is not of great value for historical events, though it can be of use for sociological study and of course for literary, theology, and other non-historical disciplines of the Hebrew Bible. The use of stereotyped and formulaic language is not unusual in chronicles, but it is a way of organizing data, not necessarily of distorting it. So far, there is good evidence that the chronicle-type material in 1 and 2 Kings is fairly reliable. Unfortunately, it usually makes up only a small part of the material in the biblical text.

Chapter 3

THE BOOKS OF KINGS AND HISTORY:
SOLOMON TO OMRI

Outline of 1 Kings 1.1 to 16.14

The contents of Solomon's reign and that of the following kings are outlined here (a form critical outline somewhat similar but with some differences in arrangement is given by Long 1984, 33-170). Parallels from 1 and 2 Chronicles are also given, because this will help us to see some important differences between the story in Kings and the story as it is narrated in Chronicles. Where one text (Kings or Chronicles) does not have a parallel to the other, this is indicated by a dash (—).

1-11 (//1 Chr. 29.20–2 Chr. 9.31): reign of Solomon.
    1.1–2.12 (//1 Chr. 29.20-30): last days of David and the coronation of Solomon.
    2.13-46 (//2 Chr. —): Solomon removes potential opposition and exacts revenge.
    3 (//2 Chr. 1.1-13): Solomon prays for wisdom and is granted it.
        3.1-15 (//2 Chr. 1.1-13): Solomon goes to Gibeon to sacrifice and pray.
        3.16-28 (//2 Chr. —): Solomon's wisdom in the case of two prostitutes.
    4.1–5.8 (//2 Chr. —): overview of Solomon's administrative arrangements.
        4.1-6: officials.
        4.7-20: twelve prefects over regime providing food for royal household.
        5.1-8: provisions for royal household and Solomon's possessions.
    5.9-14 (//2 Chr. —): Solomon's wisdom.
    5.15–8.66 (//2 Chr. 2.1–7.10): building programme.
        5.15-32 (//2 Chr. 2.1-17: arrangements with Hiram, king of Tyre.
            5.27-32: stones quarried and timber cut with corvée labour.
        6 (//2 Chr. 3.1-14): building of House to Yhwh.
        7.1-12 (//2 Chr. —): building of Solomon's palace.
            7.2-7: building of House of Lebanon Forest.
            7.8: building of Solomon's residence, house for Pharaoh's daughter.
        7.13-47 (//2 Chr. 3.15–4.19): Hiram, Tyrian coppersmith, makes bronze
                equipment for temple.
        7.48-51 (//2 Chr. 4.20–5.1): gold vessels made and deposited in temple, with
                gifts of David.

8.1-66 (//2 Chr. 5.2–7.10): temple dedicated.
    8.1-11: Ark of Covenant brought into temple; cloud of Yhwh's presence
        fills temple.
    8.12-64: Solomon's prayer, blessing, sacrifices.
    8.65-66: feast kept for 7 days, then 7 days—14 days (in 8th month).
9.1-9 (//2 Chr. 7.11-22): Yhwh appears to Solomon a second time, with promise
    of establishing throne.
9.10-14 (//2 Chr. 8.1-4): Solomon gives Hiram, king of Tyre, towns in the
    Galilee.
9.15-24 (//2 Chr. 8.5-11): Solomon uses corvée labour for various building
    projects.
9.25 (//2 Chr. 8.12-16): Solomon offers sacrifices three times a year.
9.26-28 (//2 Chr. 8.17-18): Solomon builds fleet at Ezion-geber to bring gold
    from Ophir.
10.1-13 (//2 Chr. 9.1-12): visit of queen of Sheba.
10.14-15 (//2 Chr. 9.13-14): vast quantity of gold received each year.
10.16-21 (//2 Chr. 9.15-20): objects made from gold for the palace.
10.22 (//2 Chr. 9.21): Solomon's Tarshish fleet.
10.23-29 (//2 Chr. 9.22-28): summary of Solomon's wealth, wisdom, splendour.
11.1-40 (//2 Chr. —): Solomon sins in his later years.
    11.1-8: love of foreign women makes Solomon honour other gods.
    11.9-40: Yhwh angry with Solomon and raises up adversaries.
        11.9-13: Yhwh will tear kingdom away, except one tribe.
        11.14-22: Hadad the 'Edomite', who takes refuge in Egypt.
        11.23-25: Rezon b. Elida flees from Hadadezer of Zobah to Damascus.
        11.26-40: Jeroboam b. Nebat over the corvée; flees to Shishak.
        11.29-36: prophet Ahijah says ten tribes torn away but one left.
11.41-43 (//2 Chr. 9.29-31): rest of acts of Solomon summarized.
12.1-24 (//2 Chr. 10.1–11.4): split of kingdom between Rehoboam and Jeroboam.
12.25–14.20 (//2 Chr. —): reign of Jeroboam I.
    12.26-33: establishes calf shrines in Dan and Bethel; also new autumn festival.
    13: episode of man of God who prophesies against Jeroboam, and old prophet.
    14.1-18: Ahijah prophesies death of Jeroboam's son and destruction of his house.
    14.19-20: summary of Jeroboam's reign.
14.21-31 (//2 Chr. 11.5–12.16): reign of Rehoboam.
— (//2 Chr. 11.5-23: Rehoboam's building, cultic, administrative programmes.)
14.25-28 (//2 Chr. 12.1-11): Shishak's invasion and spoiling of Jerusalem.
15.1-8 (2 Chr. 13.1-23): reign of Abijam (Abijah in 2 Chronicles) over Jerusalem.
15.6 (2 Chr. —): war between Abijam and Jeroboam all their days.
— (2 Chr. 13.2-19: Abijah defeats Jeroboam in battle.)
— (2 Chr. 13.20-21: Abijah grows strong; has many wives, sons.)
15.9-24 (2 Chr. 14.1-15.24): reign of Asa.
15.11-12 (2 Chr. 14.1-4): Asa does good: expels *qĕdēšîm*, removes idols.
— (2 Chr. 14.5-14: fortifies cities, military; defeats invading Zerah the Cushite.)
— (2 Chr. 15.1-15: heeds prophecy of Azariah (Oded?); assembles people and
    makes covenant to worship Yhwh.
15.13 (2 Chr. 15.16): deposes Maacah from being queen mother; removes
    Asherah.

15.14 (2 Chr. 15.17): *bāmôt* allowed to remain.
15.15 (2 Chr. 15.18): brought consecrated objects into temple.
15.16-22 (2 Chr. 15.19–16.6): war between Asa and Baasha; Asa hires
            Ben-Hadad of Damascus to break siege of Ramah.
— (2 Chr. 16.7-10: negative prophecy of Hanani, rejected by Asa.)
15.25-31 (//2 Chr. —): reign of Nadab Jeroboam's son.
   15.27-30: Baasha conspires against Nadab at Gibbethon of Philistines and kills
            all of Jeroboam's house.
15.32–16.7 (//2 Chr. —): reign of Baasha.
   16.1-4: prophecy of Jehu against Baasha: his house to be wiped out.
   16.7: repetition of Jehu's prophecy.
16.8-14 (//2 Chr. —): reign of Elah son of Baasha.
   16.9-10: Baasha's officer Zimri kills him in Tirzah.
16.11-20 (//2 Chr. —): reign of Zimri.
   16.11-13: destroys house of Baasha.
   16.15-16: Omri acclaimed king of Israel by troops.
   16.17-19: Omri besieges Tirzah and Zimri commits suicide.

Reign of Solomon (1 Kings 1–11)

The reign of Solomon was treated as history in many discussions in the past, but this often depended on a strange definition of history. As argued above (pp. 8-14), a modern definition of history would exclude 1 Kings 1–11, though there might well be historical details within it.

*The Concept of Royal Narrative (*Königsnovelle*)*

I would argue that the Solomon story is a type of *Königsnovelle* (p. 20), using the term in a somewhat wider sense than that confined to Egyptian royal inscriptions. Some have argued that the *Königsnovelle* is not a genre (Van Seters 1983, 160-64), but even if not a formal genre, it is a recognizable type of story of which there are a number of examples. My definition includes such examples as the Alexander Romance, the Ninus and Semiramis legend, the story of Sesostris, and the Nebuchadnezzar legend as supposedly given by Abydenus (quoted in Eusebius, *Prep. evang.* 9.41.1). Note that the term 'romance' in ancient literature does not just mean a love story (though it can include such stories) but the experiences and actions of heroes and heroines, whether adventures, adversities, voyages, military campaigns, exotic experiences, or erotic encounters.

Although these examples are known from Greek literature, they are in some cases solidly based on Near Eastern romances or legends. For example, it seems clear that the Sesostris story, which is found in Herodotus (2.102-10) and Diodorus (1.53-58), is a translation and adaptation of an ancient Near Eastern model. This does not mean that either Herodotus or Diodorus knew Egyptian or got their information from Egyptian writings.

Yet they could be passing on stories that reached them in oral form, such as from Egyptian priests (whom Herodotus talked to, evidently in Greek [2.99.1-2]).

With regard to Sesostris, probably the best overview of the subject is by Alan B. Lloyd (1988, 16-37). The most important source is Herodotus who describes the deeds of an Egyptian king called *Sesōstris* (2.102-11). As with most of the pharaohs Herodotus's chronology is vague, but the king is said to have done a number of great deeds. Most of them have to do with military expeditions and conquests (e.g. he subdued all the peoples through Asia as far as Europe, as well as those who dwelled by the Red Sea), but there were other deeds: he made captives of his campaigns drag blocks of stone to build the temple at Hephaestus and dig canals; divided the land and gave an equal parcel to each Egyptian; established a yearly tax on the land; was the only Egyptian king who also ruled Ethiopia, setting up statues of himself and his family before the temple of Hephaestus to commemorate this. The *Aegyptiaca* of the native Egyptian priest Manetho (Waddell 1940, 70-73) also describes a campaign of Sesostris as far as Thrace. Diodorus Siculus likewise gives a version but in much more elaborated and legendary form. Yet most features of the story in Diodorus are parallel to those in Herodotus and appear to be capable of explanation as a mere elaboration of Herodotus.

In sum, what can we say about the Sesostris story? Is it history? The answer is that it has a historical core (from combined traditions of the three pharaohs named Senwosret or Senusret [*S-n-wsr.t*], all of the 12th Dynasty in the Middle Kingdom early in the second millennium BCE), but many of the details are not historical. The important thing is the literary model that has important parallels to the Solomon story.

The Ninus/Semiramis legend was also widespread in the Hellenistic Near East but is best attested in the version of Diodorus of Sicily (2.1-20). Whatever Diodorus's source (which is generally thought to be Ctesias of Cnidus, who is notoriously unreliable), the story relates to great military exploits, first by Ninus (e.g. conquering all of Asia except Bactria and India) and then by Semiramis after his death. There are also magnificent building projects: Nineveh (founded by Ninus) and Babylon (founded by Semiramis). As a close study of the detailed exploits shows, a number of the deeds performed have a close parallel in events in Alexander's conquests.

The Near Eastern origin of the hero tales is in part confirmed by what happened to their development. As time went on, the original hero stories were expanded and elaborated on in their Greek context, as described above. However, in their Greek milieu something else happened as well:

they became romances (see especially Perry 1967; Braun 1938). There is an interesting parallel to this in the Moses story. Even Moses becomes a warrior hero figure like Sesostris, Ninus, and Alexander. One story makes him an Egyptian general who defeated the Ethiopians in battle, according to some Hellenistic Jewish writers. Elements of romance are also included in that he marries the daughter of the Ethiopian king (Artapanus, as preserved in Eusebius, *Praep. evang.* 9.27.1-37).

This has been only a brief survey of some of the legends about royal figures (or *Königsnovellen*) extant in the Hellenistic Near East (but going back in some cases to pre-Greek legends). Yet the parallels are sufficient to indicate the type of story that we find in the account of Solomon's reign in 1 Kings. This has significant implications for the question of historicity with regard to the Solomon story.

Solomon's Reign

1 Kings 1 seems to begin in the wrong place. It appears to be giving the final part of David's reign. Indeed, some manuscripts of the LXX attach 3 Kgdms 1.1–2.11 to 2 Kingdoms 24–26 and begin 3 Kingdoms only after David's death (that is, at MT 2 Kgs 2.12). Yet the story does begin with (Hebrew) 1 Kings 1 in a sense because the account of how David declared Solomon to be king is essential to the transition from David's reign to Solomon's. Solomon's reign began in violence, because there were rival claims by older brothers, but this was typical for new kings through much of history. Often there were rivals or potential rivals for the throne, and the new king had to deal with this problem. The story of Solomon's first couple of years is the story of his driving out the competition or potential competition, sometimes 'with extreme prejudice'.

Once past this violent consolidation of his throne, the narrative about the whole of Solomon's reign (1 Kgs 2–11) seems to be rather different from those about Saul and David. One is immediately struck by how uniform it is. Although the text shows signs of editing (for there are some repetitions and signs of unevenness), it is essentially a folktale about an Oriental potentate—it is a royal legend or *Königsnovelle*. Although the story of David has him expanding his territory via conquests, there is nothing to suggest that he rules all the land between Egypt and the Euphrates, yet this is the territory that Solomon controls, even though he fought no battles (1 Kgs 5.1, 4). There is not a hint that David could monopolize the trade in horses between Egypt and Mesopotamia (1 Kgs 10.28-29). As for the wealth invested in the House for Yhwh, this is commensurate with the quantity of gold that Solomon receives each year: 666 talents plus the revenue from trade, etc. (1 Kgs 10.14-15). Only a great empire, such as that of the later Persians, could collect so much wealth: according to Herodotus (3.91) the Persians collected 14,560 talents of silver in tribute annually— the equivalent of 1120 talents of gold. The idea that Solomon could raise 666 talents of gold plus much additional wealth each year is a gross flight of fancy on the part of the writer. In this story, though, the height of marvels is Solomon's great wisdom (1 Kgs 10.3, 6-8, 23-24), though we are given little in the way of examples of how this is demonstrated.

The episode relating to the queen of Sheba illustrates the historical problem (1 Kgs 10.1-13). Although I have characterized the Solomon story on the whole as an 'Oriental tale', the Sheba story is one of the most stereotypical: it can be characterized as a *legend*. A legend is a story, but one that focuses on the 'wondrous, miraculous, and exemplary'. The story has all the marks of a folk tale (though it has been incorporated into the text by a literary writer). The main figure has no name: she is simply 'the queen of Sheba'. She herself is a representative of wealth, wisdom, and power. Yet her function in the story is to marvel at all that Solomon and Jerusalem have to show her: in spite of all her own wealth and wisdom, Solomon's are much greater. He leaves her speechless.

The queen of Sheba story is often defended as historical by explaining it as a journey to establish trade relations between southern Arabia and Israel (e.g. Malamat 1982, 191, 204; Kitchen 1997), yet the biblical text says not a word about such a purpose. On the contrary, according to 1 Kgs 10.1, the queen of Sheba came to Solomon 'to test him with riddles'. Attempts have been made to authenticate the story by appealing to developments in southern Arabia by the tenth century. However, Mario Liverani encapsulates the problem in a nutshell:

> It was easy to decorate details that were otherwise authentic, but far more banal, with colourful fictional features. For examples, opening up trading links with the Yemen in the tenth century is not anachronistic; but the story of the Queen of Sheba's visit is too much like a fairy-tale in style and in use of narrative themes to be regarded as anything other than a romance from the Persian era. (Liverani 2005, 315)

This becomes even clearer when we consider the archaeology.

Archaeology of Solomon's Kingdom
Only a brief summary of Jerusalem can be given here; for further infor-mation, see Grabbe 2007b, 65-77. Since Jerusalem is probably the most contested site in Palestine, the main question is what kind of a settlement the city was in Iron Age IIA (often equated with the age of Solomon).

Was it a minor settlement, perhaps a large village or possibly a citadel but not a city, or was it the capital of a flourishing—or at least an emerging—state? D.W. Jamieson-Drake (1991) was one of the first who queried the status of Jerusalem, concluding that it did not have the characteristics of a capital city, including monumental architecture, until the eighth century BCE. Jamieson-Drake has been rightly criticized for lacks in his data, but it seems that he was correct in his general conclusions as far as he went, though he gave an incomplete description (Steiner 2001, 284).

Excavations on the Ophel (the area between the City of David and the temple area) show the earliest buildings there date only from the ninth century. Eilat Mazar had argued that the fortified complex of this area south of the Temple Mount had been constructed as early as the ninth century, but they more likely date between the eighth and the early sixth centuries BCE (Killebrew 2003, 336). Also, the elaborate water system of Middle Bronze IIB (eighteenth–seventeenth centuries BCE) went out of use until the eighth/seventh centuries (Warren's shaft never served as a water system), as shown by the excavations of Reich and Shukron (Killebrew 2003, 334-35). Mazar describes what she refers to as 'Solomon's wall' (2011). There is some discrepancy between her original dating of the pottery to the eighth century and her more recent dating to the tenth century. Killebrew refers to an eighth- to early sixth-century BCE dating for the building complex (2003, 336). It seems clear that relating these finds to Solomon's time is very uncertain.

Recent studies have drawn attention to two major contradictions between the biblical account and Jerusalem of the tenth century BCE. The first argues that rather than being a great city, the capital of a far-flung empire, the 'paucity of remains from this time slot in the City of David does not allow one to assume that the population of the city exceeded 2,000' (Geva 2014). This agrees with an earlier assessment by Margreet Steiner (2001, 2003): Jerusalem of the tenth and ninth centuries was a small town occupied mainly by public buildings, not exceeding 12 hectares and approximately 2,000 inhabitants.

As for the second point, the argument that the Middle Bronze wall was used as a city wall in the LB, Iron I, and Iron IIA and IIB has no archaeo-logical support: Jerusalem lacked a fortification wall until the mid-eighth century when the MB IIB wall was partially built over and partially reused for a new fortification wall (Killebrew 2003, 334; Ussishkin 2003, 110-11). The lack of other finds relating to fortification suggests that Jerusalem was unwalled and unfortified between the LB and Iron IIB (sixteenth to mid-eighth century), and thus Jerusalem was 'at best modest' (Killebrew 2003, 334). This of course differs from the picture of the text.

Yet it is supported by a recent study by Doron Ben-Ami which argued that excavations at the Givati parking lot (southwest of the Temple Mount) showed that there were no Iron IIA fortifications on the southeast ridge ('City of David' settlement); rather, 'all Iron Age fortification components unearthed in Jerusalem are the outcome of one comprehensive building operation that took place at the close of the 8th century BCE' (Ben-Ami 2014, 17).

The Question of Historicity
N. Na'aman (1997) analyzed the account of Solomon for the existence of sources. He accepts that the early 'chronicle of Israelite kings' was created in the eighth century and thus rather later than Solomon; however, the Deuteronomist also had the 'Book of the Acts of Solomon' (1 Kgs 11.41), which Na'aman tries to reconstruct. Some episodes were invented by the post-Dtr redactor, including the queen of Sheba and the description of the temple (based on a description of the temple of his own times). Na'aman concludes that only in the late redaction do we have a picture of a ruler of an empire and a great sage. Although I agree that there was a *Chronicle of the Kings of Judah* (see Chapter 2, pp. 21-28), I am more sceptical of a 'Book of the Acts of Solomon'. Were such writings being produced this early? Administrative documents, yes, but not the sort of biographical writing envisaged here (see further Grabbe 2007b, 115-18).

In a long survey of the Solomonic tradition M. H. Niemann (1997) argues that Solomon's alleged building programme of cities and monumental buildings cannot be confirmed archaeologically. Instead, we find evidence of a series of representatives (often relatives) who were sent to the northern areas as the first attempt to build a network of loyalty in an area that had not yet declared for Solomon's rule. Solomon might have indeed married the daughter of an Egyptian pharaoh, but this would have been because he was a vassal of that pharaoh (Shoshenq?). This could be the reason that Jerusalem is not found on the Shoshenq inscription. E.A. Knauf (1997) thinks that Solomon was historical but that he differed considerably from the biblical picture. The king's name shows that he was non-Judaean in origin ('Solomon' comes from Shalim/Shalem, the old god of the pre-Israelite inhabitants of Jerusalem). The Bathsheba story was not suppressed because there was a worse story: Solomon was not David's! Solomon was the son of a Jerusalem mother but not necessarily of a Judaean father. He became king through a *coup d'état* by getting rid of the Jerusalem elite. He was no monotheist, because the Judaean tribal deity Yhwh had only a subordinate position in the Jerusalem pantheon.

These are three examples of scholars who accept the existence of Solomon but reject the biblical image of a great empire or a powerful ruler over a major state. Solomon simply consolidated what David had conquered and apparently managed to rule peaceably (at least for most of his reign) over a small polity in central Palestine. The reality had little to do with the later legend. Thus, here and there might be a verse that reflects the historical Solomon, but to my mind the Solomon story is the most problematic of 1 and 2 Kings, providing the thickest cloud of obscurity over the history that lies behind it.

Invasion of Shishak (Shoshenq I: 1 Kings 14.25-28)

According to 1 Kgs 14.25-28 a king Shishak of Egypt came up against Jerusalem in Rehoboam's 5th year and took all the treasures of the temple. When an inscription of Shoshenq I (ca. 945–920 BCE), founder of the 22nd Dynasty, was deciphered at Karnak listing many topographical sites in Palestine, a connection was made with the passage in the Bible and has been the standard view ever since. His dates of reign vary among specialists; as for his campaign to Palestine it has recently been dated to about 925 or 924 BCE (Jansen-Winkeln 2006), but another dating attempt puts it in 917 BCE (Shortland 2005). All seem to agree that Shoshenq's expedition was a signal event in Israel's history, but precisely what happened on the ground and even when the invasion took place is considerably disputed. The conventional view is heavily informed by the Bible. According to it, Shoshenq's army made a number of destructive raids on various parts of Palestine, destroying many sites in the Negev and even as far north as Megiddo; however, Jerusalem did not fall because the Pharaoh was bought off by Rehoboam.

A number of studies have addressed the issue of Israel/Judah and Shoshenq's 'invasion', beginning with M. Noth's study in 1938 (for a survey of earlier studies, see Wilson 2005; also Schipper 1999, 119-32; Ash 1999, 50-56). Most have assumed that Shoshenq conducted an invasion of Palestine, that the inscription gives some sort of invasion route, that the inscription can be reconciled with the biblical text, and that the archaeology matches the inscription. There have, nevertheless, been some problems, especially the fact that Israel and Judah are not mentioned specifically, that no site in Judah occurs in the inscription, that the toponyms cannot be worked into any sort of itinerary sequence, and that the biblical text says nothing about an invasion of the Northern Kingdom.

It might not be surprising that a Jerusalem scribe did not record the details of Shoshenq's raids on Israel, but why omit the destructive attacks on the Negev, which was a part of Judah—at least, in the eyes of the Bible? Leaving aside the Jerusalem question, there is still considerable disagreement how to interpret Shoshenq's inscription. Was it a raid or primarily an occupation—albeit temporary—of the land? Various explanations have been given of the order of toponyms as they might relate to the progress of the invasion, but none has been completely convincing. Now, however, Kevin Wilson (2005) has investigated Shoshenq's inscription in the context of other Egyptian triumphal inscriptions. He concludes:

- Triumphal inscriptions were designed to extol the Pharaoh's exploits, not provide historical data.
- The reliefs glorify all the exploits of the king rather than a particular campaign.
- The topographical lists are not laid out according to any system that allows a reconstruction of the military route.
- The sites listed may in some cases be those attacked, but others not attacked—indeed, friendly towns and allies—might be listed as well.
- The lists were apparently drawn in part from military records and onomastical lists (lists of topographical or other names), which means that some data of value for certain purposes may be included.

The implications of these conclusions are considerable. Rather than recording a particular campaign into Palestine, Shoshenq's inscription may include more than one (as maintained by Knauf 2008). This would help to explain the vague nature of the inscriptions that accompany the topographical lists, without clarifying the reasons for or objectives of the 'invasion'. In any case, the precise nature and progress of the campaign(s) cannot be worked out.

More puzzling is the lack of any reference to Judah or Jerusalem as such. The argument is that this was in a section of the inscription that is no longer readable. This argument is still maintained by the latest study of the Shoshenq inscription by Wilson (2005). It must be said that this argument, while possible, is not compelling. Another obvious interpretation is that Shoshenq bypassed Judah—or at least, the Judaean highlands—because it did not suit his purpose, and the biblical writer got it wrong (see the suggestion of Niemann in the previous section). Interestingly, the solution that seems to be agreed on by both A. Mazar (2008, 107-10) and

I. Finkelstein et al. (2008, 37-39) is that Shoshenq was indeed interested in coming up against Judah because of the copper trade. This could make Jerusalem not just a stage in the invasion but its main object (though not Finkelstein's view). This is an interesting interpretation, though one might ask why Shoshenq then pushed on north as far as the Jezreel Valley if he had already reached his objective.

Finkelstein et al. (2008) argue that the main phase of prosperity was post-Shoshenq and that the sites in the south were primarily not destroyed but abandoned. They point out that Shoshenq also does not mention the Philistine cities, which could be significant. They interpret it as evidence for their control of the copper trade. But whether or not that is right, we have to ask why the Philistines were omitted. If the Egyptian expedition was a general attack on Palestinian cities in Israel and Judah, why should the area of the Philistine plain be omitted? Could these cities have a particular relationship with Egypt? Or was the Shoshenq operation a more complex one? David Ussishkin (2008, 205-6) makes the reasonable argument that Shoshenq would hardly set up his stela in a ruined city, but suggests that Megiddo was not just attacked but was occupied to become a regional headquarters. To me, this calls for a rethink of how destructive Shoshenq's raid was, as opposed to being merely for reasons of dominance and intimidation.

A final question is when this raid took place. The biblical text places it under Rehoboam, but some have wanted to put it earlier, under Solomon's time (see the discussion and references in Finkelstein 2002, 110; see also Niemann 1997, 297-99). The problem is that the date of Shoshenq's campaign, its precise nature, and the dating of Solomon's rule all contribute to a great deal of uncertainty.

Split of the Kingdom under Rehoboam and Jeroboam
(1 Kings 12–14)

According to the surface picture of the biblical story, a single nation of Israel split into two rival nations because of petty issues under Solomon's son Rehoboam and his non-royal opponent Jeroboam. More careful consideration of the geo-political facts, as well as a number of biblical passages that are easily overlooked, shows that the union of two ethnic groups under David was an artificial one. It is obvious historically that both Judah and Israel each had its own national identity and was separate from and a rival of the other from an early period, as can be briefly noted: in one of the earliest passages in the Hebrew Bible (Judg. 5) Judah is not even mentioned in this early poem which names most of the tribes; elsewhere in Judges Judah is seldom mentioned with other tribes (for example, in Judg. 1, Judah takes Simeon with them in conquering their territory [1.3, 17], but Simeon then disappears from the text); David ruled first over Judah alone for seven years (2 Sam. 2.11). Judah was originally separate and only later added artificially to the list of Israelite tribes.

Inevitable strains would no doubt at some point have led to a reversion to the original separate political entities. The surprise was that the unity lasted not only through the reign of David but also through that of Solomon. Whatever his faults, Solomon managed to keep the country together throughout his monarchy. Thus, although there had not been a United Monarchy as depicted in the biblical text, a union of sorts had been effected by David and kept in place by his successor. Yet Solomon had evidently got the backs up of many people because of his administrative burdens; one can assume that heavy taxes was one of these. We know about these tensions from the demands made by the people to Rehoboam, 'Your father made harsh our yoke: now if you lighten your father's hard service and the heavy yoke that he imposed on us, we shall serve you' (1 Kgs 12.4).

According to the biblical story, Rehoboam ignored the advice of the elders, which was to accommodate the reasonable demands of the people, and followed the advice of his young advisors who wanted him to give a brutal reply to them. Although we cannot be confident of the details, the split of the kingdom back into Judah and Israel after Solomon's death seems to be correctly remembered by the text. The rule of Solomon's son Rehoboam was accepted by Judah, but Israel chose to go with Jeroboam as ruler: he is represented as having been in charge of corvée labour during part of Solomon's reign.

Reign of Abijam and Asa of Judah (1 Kings 15.1-24)

The rule of Abijam, son of Rehoboam, in Jerusalem is essentially a blank. We learn only that his mother was Maacah and that he reigned three years. The war with Jeroboam, begun under his father, continued. Otherwise, all we have are the standard Deuteronomistic statements made about every king of the Northern Kingdom and most kings of Judah that he was wicked. We do not even know whether his successor Asa was his son or his brother: 1 Kgs 15.8 says Asa was Abijam's son, but his mother was the same as Abijam's (1 Kgs 15.10; the word for 'father' [*'āv*] and 'brother' [*'āḥ*] are similar in Hebrew).

The short description of Asa's reign focuses on his righteousness, but the question is how much of the data might have come from an official chronicle, as opposed to the contribution of the Deuteronomist who was interpreting any information from a source and also making theological statements and judgments. The following *could* have come from an official annal, because they are the sort of things that a court chronicle might well record:

- Deposed the queen mother (Maacah who was his mother or possibly his grandmother).
- Deposited his father's and his own votive objects in the temple.
- Bribed the Aramaean Bar-Hadad son of Tabrimmon son of Hezion to attack Israel (so Baasha would cease to build Ramah that blocked movement from Judah to the north).
- Built Geba and Mizpah of Benjamin.
- Had an ailment in his feet.

The removal of the queen mother is a unique event in biblical history, partly because it is the only passage talking about a queen mother. If the queen mother had an official function in the Judahite monarchy, we have no information on it. According to the Deuteronomist's theological interpretation, she was removed from office because she made a cult object for Asherah. This appears prima facie unlikely, since it has recently become acknowledged that according to Israelite belief Yhwh had a female consort, Asherah. This female 'partner' was eventually dropped, but that apparently did not happen until the seventh century, several centuries after Asa. Thus, the statement that the queen mother was removed because of making an Asherah cult object is likely to be a Deuteronomistic interpretation rather than information from a chronicle. The same judgment applies to Asa's removing the *qᵉdēšîm* from the land. This term has often been translated as 'male cult prostitute', but this is now generally rejected: there is little or no evidence of cult prostitution (whether male or female) in Canaanite religion, as was once assumed. (On these points relating to religion, see further in Chapter 6, pp. 86-90 below.)

The information on bribing Bar-Hadad looks more authentic. The question is whether Israelite territory extended this far north at that time. Thus, the Deuteronomist might have had useful information, but it is also possible that he is creating a scenario from knowledge of Israelite territory at a later time. Our problem is that our knowledge of the Aramaean kingdoms that dominated Syrian history in the first millennium BCE is defective, which often makes difficult judging biblical statements on the question. There is also the matter of Asa's defeating Zerah the Cushite ('Ethiopian'), though this episode is found only in 2 Chr. 14.8-14 and is absent from 1 Kings. Some have tried to defend this as authentic even though the DtrH of Kings knows nothing about it. It was once suggested that 'Zerah' was a reflex of the name of Pharaoh Ororkon I who lived about this time, but Egyptian philologists now refute any connection between the names. The name is neither Nubian nor Egyptian but biblical: Gen. 36.17; Josh. 7.1; 1 Chr. 1.37; Neh. 11.24. The Egyptologist B.U. Schipper examined the story in the light of biblical and Egyptian considerations and concluded that 2 Chr. 14.8-14 is 'in no way a historical document from the ninth century but an example of Old Testament theology from the post-exilic period' (1999, 133-39, quote translated from p. 139).

Rulers of Israel to Omri (1 Kings 15.25–16.20)

Several short-lived rulers of the Northern Kingdom filled in the time between Jeroboam and Omri; the only one who ruled for any length of time was Baasha. First, Nadab the son of Jeroboam ruled for two years (1 Kgs 15.25-31). All we know of him is that while laying siege to Gibbethon in Philistia, he was struck down by Baasha. Baasha then proceeded to kill all members of Jeroboam's house (1 Kgs 15.29-30). Baasha ruled 24 years, and there is a fair amount of text on his rule (1 Kgs 15.27-30, 32-34; 16.1-6), yet we know little about him other than that he began to build Ramah and that his house was destroyed, like that of Jeroboam. Baasha was succeeded by his son Elah (1 Kgs 16.8-14) who ruled two years. His chariot commander Zimri killed him while he was drinking in the capital Tirzah and then proceeded to kill all males of the house of Baasha. But Zimri lasted only seven days, because the army chose their commander Omri who then besieged Zimri in Tirzah, and the latter committed suicide (1 Kgs 16.15-20). Omri consolidated his rule by defeating a rival Tibni who also had a following among the people (1 Kgs 16.21-22). Thus, Omri became king only 50 years after the death of Solomon, if the figures of the MT can be trusted.

Summary and Conclusions

This chapter covered the reign of Solomon and the half century from his reign to the beginning of Omri's, though Solomon's reign took up most of our attention. There is a reason for this: almost from start to finish Solomon fits the image of the great 'Oriental emperor'. He controls a vast territory and possesses great wealth, with absolute sovereignty over his subjects. Of course, he marries the daughter of a country of similar power—suggesting equality with Egypt in this case—and harnesses the best craftsmen and materials from legendary Tyre to build his city. His capital city consists of great palaces and a magnificent temple, with gold like dust and silver so abundant it is of little account. His household overflows with luxuries, his table groans under the weight of exotic fruits, meats from rare animals, and every sort of desirable food for consumption. His wisdom is legendary, and he exceeds all others in intellectual skills. His reputation reaches far and wide, and rulers from distant lands travel to see such a supreme example of power, wealth, and wisdom—only to find that the reports were understated! His ships travel to the ends of the earth for rare and astonishing goods.

It is difficult to discover much in the Solomon story that strikes one as likely to be historical. To conclude that a king named Solomon existed is not a problem.

His name echoing the old god of Jerusalem (Shalim/Shalem) is suggestive of reality rather than simply the piety of the David story. Here and there are data that may have come from documents in the archives or other sources. Also, he began his reign with the bloody elimination of rivals, though the idea that he took his throne in the midst of adversity which he overcame could be a part of the stereotype, and the writer probably saw nothing bad in this. Overall, I can find little in the Solomon story that looks on the face of it to be historically reliable.

Yet I am intrigued by the story that he built the Jerusalem temple. This sort of story is what we might expect, and the description of the wealth and rare construction of the temple fits well the legend. Yet David—the expected temple-builder—did not construct it, and we find nothing in the stories of the later kings that might hide such a building (with the possible exception of Jehoash who is said to collect money to repair the temple: 2 Kgs 12). This suggests that a temple was built in Jerusalem at a fairly early time. If David did not build it, who? It is likely that here we have a genuine remembrance that has been expanded into a great legend. The general description of the building's shape may well be correct, but of course it has been stylized by expanding the account and adding costly materials, such as gold, expensive wood, and the like.

We have no extra-biblical information on the splitting of the kingdom under Rehoboam and Jeroboam, and it is difficult to verify the details. Yet there are two factors that suggest the biblical account embodies events, at least in outline. First, we have clear evidence of two kingdoms in Palestine, the Kingdom of Israel and the Kingdom of Judah. We also have evidence that this division between Judah and Israel was a long-standing situation:

what was unusual was that they were temporarily united under a single ruler in the time of David and Solomon. The second factor confirming the situation is that it leads up to Omri and Ahab who are known from inscriptions of surrounding nations. Thus, even though we cannot confirm that any of the figures in the text actually existed, possessed the names alleged for them, or carried out the events described, we can be confident that possibly at the end of Solomon's life, but most likely after his death, the polity over which he ruled reverted to its natural division into two communities.

These two communities had much in common in language and culture, including religion. But there was no reason why they should be united politically or have the same ruler. The distance from Solomon to Omri is a very short period of time. It appears that the text has embedded in it a correct memory of some of the rulers and their interactions that filled in this chronological period. But just as much in the Solomon story is not credible, we also cannot confirm all the details in 1 Kings 12–16. Historical data are certainly present in the writings, but the text has to be investigated carefully and critically in order to extract it.

Chapter 4

The Books of Kings and History: The Omride Dynasty and Rulers to the Fall of Samaria

Outline of 1 Kings 16 to 2 Kings 17

Here is an outline of the contents (for a form critical outline, see Long 1984, 165-242; 1991, 7-190). Parallels from 2 Chronicles are also listed (where Kings or Chronicles omit material found in the other, a dash [—] is given to show the lack of material).

1 Kgs 16.15-28 (//2 Chr. —): the reign of Omri.
    16.15-20: Zimri reigns seven days in Tirzeh after a coup but is defeated by the army commander Omri and commits suicide.
    16.21-22: the people split between Omri and Tibni, but Omri kills Tibni in battle.
    16.23-24: Omri reigns 12 years, buys a hill and founds the city of Samaria.
    16.25-28: Omri's reign given a theological summary without additional information.
1 Kgs 16.29-34 (//2 Chr. —): a theologizing summary of Ahab's reign.
    16.29-33: Ahab reigns 22 years, marries Jezebel, worships Baal, builds Baal temple.
    16.34: Hiel builds Jericho at the expense of his first born and youngest sons.
1 Kgs 17–19 (//2 Chr. —): various tales centring on Elijah the prophet/man of God.
    17.1-6: Elijah declares a famine to Ahab, then hides where he is fed by ravens.
    17.7-16: Elijah lives with a widow where they are fed miraculously.
    17.17-24: Elijah heals/raises to life the son of the widow.
    18: Elijah's contest with the prophets of Baal and the end of the drought.
    19.1-14: Elijah flees to Horeb from the wrath of Jezebel.
    19.15-18: Elijah is sent to anoint Hazael, Jehu, and Elisha.
    19.19-21: Elisha leaves his farming to follow Elijah.
1 Kgs 20 (//2 Chr. —): Ahab and the attack of the Aramaeans.
    20.1-21: Ben-Hadad threatens Ahab but is defeated by Israel at the word of a prophet.
    20.22-30: the prophet warns of a second invasion, but Aramaeans defeated at the word of a man of God.

20.31-34: Ben-Hadad surrenders to Ahab who spares his life; Ben-Hadad
promises to return the towns taken from Ahab's
father by his father, and to let Israel set up bazaars in
Damascus as his father did in Samaria.

20.35-43: a prophet appears to Ahab as a sign of his error in releasing
Ben-Hadad.

1 Kgs 21 (//2 Chr. —): Ahab and Naboth's vineyard.

21.1-16: Ahab takes Naboth's vineyard.

21.17-26: Elijah prophesies against Ahab and his house.

21.27-29: Ahab repents and the prophecy against him is postponed to his son's
time.

— (//2 Chr. 17: reign of Jehoshaphat.)

— (//2 Chr. 17.2: fortified cities and deputies in captured cities of Ephraim.)

— (//2 Chr. 17.3-6: Jehoshaphat's piety.)

— (//2 Chr. 17.7-9: sends official, Levites, priests to teach the Torah in the land.)

— (//2 Chr. 17.10-19: other nations make peace; Jehoshaphat's officers, military
power.)

— (//2 Chr. 18.1: Jehoshaphat makes marriage alliance with Ahab.)

1 Kgs 22 (//2 Chr. 18): story of Ahab's death.

22.1-5 (//2 Chr. 18.2-4): Ahab asks Jehoshaphat for help in retaking
Ramoth-gilead.

22.6-28 (//2 Chr. 18.5-27): prophets consulted; Micaiah prophesies defeat.

22.29-38 (//2 Chr. 18.28-34): Ahab killed in battle, fulfilling Yhwh's word.

22.39-40 (//2 Chr. —): summary of Ahab's reign, including his 'ivory house'.

22.41-51//2 Chr. 20.31–21.3): summary of Jehoshaphat's reign, including his
'righteousness' and his failed plan to send ships of
Tarshish to Ophir for gold.

22.52-54 (//2 Chr. —): Ahaziah son of Ahab becomes king and reigns two years.

2 Kgs 1 (//2 Chr. —): Ahaziah dies at the word of Elijah for enquiring of
Baal-zebub (most of the chapter concerns the efforts
to get Elijah to come to visit the king on his sick
bed).

2 Kgs 2 (//2 Chr. —): Elijah is taken to heaven and Elisha assumes his mantle.

2 Kgs 3 (//2 Chr. —): coalition of kings attack Moab.

3.1-3: Jehoram becomes king over Israel.

3.4-9: Mesha the king of Moab rebels against Jehoram who assembles coalition
of Israel, Judah, and Edom.

3.9-20: the kings are delivered from lack of water by Elisha.

3.21-27: Moab defeated but Israel withdraws after Mesha sacrifices crown
prince.

2 Kgs 4.1–8.15 (//2 Chr. —): tales about Elisha.

4: various tales of Elisha.

5: Elisha heals Naaman the Aramaean commander.

6.1-7: Elisha makes an axehead float.

6.8-23: Elisha delivers Aramaean army to Israel; and the Aramaeans stop
invading.

6.24–7.20: Ben-Hadad besieges Samaria, but Aramaeans flee; Elisha delivers
city.

8.1-6: Elisha helps woman whose son he had revived.

8.7-15: Elisha prophesies Hazael will replace Ben-Hadad; former assassinates latter.

2 Kgs 8.16-24 (//2 Chr. 21.4-11; 21.20–22.1): summary of the reign of Joram son of Jehoshaphat over Judah: marries Athaliah, daughter of Ahab; Edom gains independence.

2 Kgs 8.25-29 (//2 Chr. 22.2-6): Joram of Judah dies; son Ahaziah reigns; Joram of Israel fights alongside Ahaziah against Hazael at Ramoth-gilead and is wounded.

2 Kgs 9–10 (2 Chr. 22.7-9): Jehu stages a coup and takes the throne.

9.1-14: Elisha sends a disciple to anoint Jehu king in Ramoth-gilead.

9.15-29 (//2 Chr. 22.7-9): Jehu kills Joram of Israel and Ahaziah of Judah.

9.30-37: Jehu kills Jezebel.

10.1-11: Jehu causes Ahab's offspring to be killed.

10.12-14: relatives of Ahaziah are killed.

10.15-17: Jehu takes Jehonadab the Rechabite to witness slaughter of Ahab's house.

10.18-28: Jehu slaughters Baal worshipers and removes Baal worship from Israel.

10.29-31: yet Jehu does not follow the Torah or remove worship at Bethel and Dan.

10.32-33: Hazael takes Israelite land east of the Jordon.

10.34-36: summary of Jehu's reign.

2 Kgs 11–12 (//2 Chr. 22.10–24.14): coup of Joash and his reign over Judah.

11 (//2 Chr. 22.10–23.21): execution of Athaliah; installation of Joash on throne.

12.1-17 (//2 Chr. 24.1-14): Joash has money collected to repair Yhwh's house.

— (//2 Chr. 24.15-22: death of high priest Jehoiada; execution of son Zechariah.)

12.18-19 (//2 Chr. 24.23-24): Hazael comes against Jerusalem; Joash buys him off.

12.20-22 (//2 Chr. 24.25-27): Joash's death and summary of his reign.

2 Kgs 13.1-9 (//2 Chr. —): reign of Jehoahaz son of Jehu.

13.1-2: summary of Jehoahaz's reign.

13.3: Israel afflicted by Hazael and Ben-Hadad of Aram.

13.4-6: Israel gains freedom from Aram despite remaining in sins of Jeroboam.

13.7: Jehoahaz had been left with only small military force.

13.8-9: Jehoahaz's death and summary of his reign.

2 Kgs 13.10-25 (//2 Chr. —): reign of Jehoash of Israel.

13.10-13: summary of Jehoash's reign.

13.14-19: Elisha on death bed offers to Jehoash a sign of defeat of Aram.

13.20-21: death of Elisha and resurrection of corpse by touch of his bones.

13.22-25: Jehoash son of Jehoahaz begins to recover territory from Ben-Hadad.

2 Kgs 14.1-22 (//2 Chr. 25.1–26.2): reign of Amaziah of Judah.

14.1-6 (//2 Chr. 25.1-4): righteous, though he did not remove country shrines.

— (//2 Chr. 25.5-10: hires Israelites but dismisses them at word of man of God.

14.7 (//2 Chr. 25.11): defeat of the Edomites.

— (//2 Chr. 25.12-16: expansion on defeat of Edomites; brings Edomite gods back and worships them; warned by prophet).

14.8-14 (//2 Chr. 25.17-24): challenges Jehoash of Israel to battle; defeated and Jerusalem sacked.

14.15-16 (//2 Chr. —): death of Jehoash of Israel and summary of his reign.

14.17-20 (//2 Chr. 25.25-28): Amaziah assassinated; summary of reign.
14.21-22 (//2 Chr. 26.1-2): Azariah (Uzziah) takes throne of Judah; restores
                Elath.
2 Kgs 14.23-29 (//2 Chr. —): reign of Jeroboam over Israel; restores territory from
                Aram.
2 Kgs 15.1-5 (//2 Chr. 26.3-23): reign of Azariah (Uzziah) over Judah; righteous.
— (//2 Chr. 26.5-20: makes conquests; develops military and agriculture;
                becomes arrogant and tries to offer incense in
                temple.)
15.6-7 (//2 Chr. 26.21-23): struck with leprosy by Yhwh; Jotham co-ruler.
2 Kgs 15.8-12 (//2 Chr. —): reign of Zechariah over Israel: assassinated, as last of
                Jehu dynasty.
2 Kgs 15.13-15 (//2 Chr. —): Shallum reigns one month.
2 Kgs 15.16-22 (//2 Chr. —): reign of Menahem over Israel; Pul of Assyria invades
                and Menahem gives him 1000 talents of silver.
2 Kgs 15.23-26 (//2 Chr. —): reign of Pekahiah of Israel.
2 Kgs 15.27-31 (//2 Chr. —): reign of Pekah of Israel; Tiglath-pileser invades and
                takes northern Israel.
2 Kgs 15.32-38 (//2 Chr. 27): reign of Jotham of Judah; attacked by Rezin of Aram
                and Pekah.
2 Kgs 16 (//2 Chr. 28): reign of Ahaz of Judah.
16.1-4 (//2 Chr. 28.1-4): theologizing summary of Ahaz's reign.
16.5-9 (//2 Chr. 28.5-19): Syro-Ephraimite war.
16.10-16 (//2 Chr. 28.20-27): Ahaz makes altar like the one of Tiglath-pileser in
                Damascus.
2 Kgs 17 (//2 Chr. —): fall of Samaria.

Omri (1 Kings 16.16-28)

From the biblical text you would be led to believe that Omri was not very
important: he has only 12 verses devoted to him. The essence of his life is
that he was the army commander declared king by the army when Zimri
assassinated Baasha. Omri established his kingdom by going against
Zimri, who committed suicide, and defeating and killing the other rival for
the throne, Tibni. Omri then purchased the hill of Shemer and founded a
new capital for the Northern Kingdom, Samaria. Otherwise, he is simply
dismissed as wicked. (For a detailed presentation of sources and a reconstruction of Omri's reign, see Grabbe 2012.)

Yet we know from Assyrian texts that Omri was a significant individual
who gave his name to his kingdom: the Assyrians long called it *Bit-Ḫumri*
('House of Omri'). The Assyrian records thus confirm the existence and
importance of Omri, though they say nothing further about him. Yet we
also find a reference to Omri in the stela left by Mesha, the king of Moab,
about 800 BCE. This 'Moabite stone' (also called 'The Mesha Stela')

states that Omri 'oppressed' Moab for his lifetime and half the lifetime of his son, 40 years, before Mesha threw off the Israelite yoke. There is a remarkable coincidence between the biblical and the extra-biblical data, as was noticed when the Moabite stone was first discovered (see further about the Moabite stone under 'Ahab').

Yet this confirmation of the biblical text has been dismissed, wrongly in my view. Is there evidence that Omri was a real person or only a personification of the state *Bit Ḥumri*? There are in fact some good examples of parallel usage in other Assyrian inscriptions. We know that Guš, the king of Yaḫan, an Aramaean state around Lake Ğabbūl in northern Syria, was an actual individual because he paid tribute to Ashurnasirpal II ca. 870 BCE (Grayson 1996, 218, lines 77-78 [text A.0.101.1]). Guš was apparently considered the founder of the state and dynasty (i.e. he is an eponym). The Zakkur Inscription lists a 'Bar-Gush' among the kings arrayed against Zakkur (A 6). Other inscriptions refer to the state or dynasty as 'house of Guš' (*Bīt-Gūsi/Bīt-Agūsi* in Assyrian [Lipiński 2000, 196 and nn.]; *byt gš* in Aramaic [*KAI* 223B: 10]).

Similarly, Hazael is clearly attested as king of Damascus in a number of Assyrian inscriptions (see below, p. 61), but after his death the land of Damascus is sometimes referred to as *Bit Hazael* in Assyrian inscriptions. Thus, we have examples in which a known historical individual (e.g. Guš, Hazael) can be taken as the founder or eponym of a dynasty, with the dynasty named after the person ('house of X') and the descendents even referred to as 'son of X'. Thus, the expression *Bīt-Ḥumri* as a reference to the state/royal house of Israel by no means rules out Omri as a historical personage. On the contrary, the Assyrian inscriptions and the Moabite stone confirm Omri's actual existence as a king of Israel.

Ahab (1 Kings 16.29–22.40)

With Ahab's reign we suddenly find ourselves with an embarrassment of riches, relatively speaking, for we have far more potential sources than for most of the Israelite and Judahite kings (for a detailed presentation of sources and a reconstruction of Ahab's reign, see Grabbe 2012). Far from removing problems and difficulties, however, they seem only to raise new ones, especially when it comes to reconciling the biblical text with the primary sources (on the concept of primary sources, see Chapter 6, pp. 82-84 below). First of all, much of the text is actually taken up with the story of Elijah the prophet, and prophetic legends cannot be taken as necessarily reliable for historical purposes, since one of their aims is to enhance the power and reputation of the prophet (see p. 20 above). Thus, Elijah is presented as opposing Jezebel single-handedly, even though the text itself admits that there were many who had not worshipped Baal (1 Kgs 19.14 vs. 19.18). Indeed, many think that the text has misrepresented the situation with Jezebel (see below and under 'Jehu').

The essential information on Ahab is summarized in a biblical passage that appears to come from a court chronicle of some sort (some editorial comments, likely expressing moral judgments by the Deuteronomist, are put in square brackets):

> Ahab son of Omri ruled over Israel in the 38th year of Asa king of Judah. Ahab son of Omri ruled over Israel in Samaria 22 years. [Ahab son of Omri did evil in the eyes of Yhwh more than all who preceded him. He made light of walking in the sin of Jeroboam son of Nebat.] And he took to wife Jezebel daughter of Ethbaal, king of the Sidonians. [He went and served Baal and worshipped him.] He set up an altar to Baal in the House of Baal which he built in Samaria. [Ahab made an Ashera, and did additional things to annoy Yhwh, the God of Israel, more than all the kings of Israel who preceded him…]. The rest of the deeds of Ahab and all that he accomplished and the house of ivory and all the cities that he built—are they not written in the Book of the Annals of the Kings of Israel? And Ahab slept with his ancestors, and Ahaziah his son ruled in his place. (1 Kgs 16.29-33; 22.39-40)

This passage illustrates our source problem. Even if we accept that the biblical text has drawn on an official chronicle, there are still problems. It is clear that we do not have the chronicle itself but an extract which has been excerpted and inserted into the biblical text, along with edits and editorial comments. For example, the bracketed material is clearly editorial material that was probably not a part of the original chronicle. Indeed, although it is not impossible that the chronicle mentioned building a temple and altar for Baal—because this would have been a factual statement—that could also be an editorial comment, as a means of condemning Ahab.

On the question of Baal, however, we have to keep in mind that the writer/editor is a later Judahite writer with a particular view of worship. At the time of Ahab both Israel and Judah were polytheistic societies. Also, the House of Baal was apparently built for Jezebel as a private royal chapel, since she herself was a Phoenician and considered Baal as her chief deity. Finally, Ahab was himself a worshipper of Yhwh. His chief palace overseer Obadiah was a devoted Yhwh worshipper, and Ahab could hardly have been ignorant of that (1 Kgs 17.3). Furthermore, his two sons had theophoric names that contained a form of the divine name

Yhwh (Ahaziah [1 Kgs 22.40] and Jehoram [2 Kgs 1.17]), which would hardly have been the case if he had been a Baal worshipper. For further information, see Chapter 6 (pp. 86-90 below).

The 'facts' of Ahab's rule seem to be the following, if we discount the theological editorializing and the various legendary accounts:

- Began his reign in the 38th year of Asa of Judah.
- Reigned 22 years.
- Married Jezebel, daughter of the king of the Sidonians.
- Built an ivory house (i.e. one housing carved ivory objects) and a number of cities.
- Built a temple to Baal, evidently for his queen Jezebel.
- 'Slept with his fathers', which implies a peaceful death.

At this point, we can consider other data in the biblical text that seem to clash with information known from extra-biblical sources. The most important contradiction in my view is that relating to the Aramaeans and Assyrians. According to the biblical text, Ahab spent his reign fighting Aramaeans (King Ben-Hadad) and was generally the underdog who came off the worse in these conflicts (see especially 1 Kgs 20 and 22). According to the extra-biblical sources it was the Assyrians that Ahab fought, and the Aramaeans were his allies. This is an essential contradiction that cannot be lightly dismissed or trivially harmonized. Of course, the Assyrian inscriptions have their own biases and interests, but modern scholars are aware of this and read them critically. The Assyrian inscriptions are important, however, because they are primary sources (on the concept of 'primary source', see Chapter 6, pp. 82-84), unlike the biblical text that was finalized long after the events. There is no question that Assyria dominated the history of the Levant at this time. Assyria was attempting to expand its tentacles toward the Mediterranean, and the small kingdoms of Syria and Palestine were in its sights. The biblical text's ignoring of the Assyrian problem is a major historical blunder that cannot be overlooked. Either the writer was grossly ignorant, or he wilfully changed the true situation, by making the Aramaeans rather than the Assyrians the enemy, for theological reasons.

The Assyrian king Shalmaneser III (858–824) marched west to make conquests in the Syrian area, beginning about 853 BCE. Shalmaneser's inscriptions show that Ahab was allied with Hadadezer of Damascus and ten other rulers in a coalition opposing the invading Assyrians at Qarqar in 853 BCE (*ANET* 278-79; also quoted in Grabbe 2007b, 131). This coalition of a dozen local kings was able to fight the Assyrians to a standoff at this time and for perhaps another dozen years. The question is, what happened between Ahab's coalition with Hadadezer of the Aramaeans of Damascus and the oppression of Israel by Hazael, which is historically atttested by primary sources? According to the biblical text Ahab fought the Aramaeans, and this seems to go contrary to the Assyrian inscriptions. But some have been willing to argue that the biblical picture is not entirely wrong. That is, Ahab's alliance with the Aramaeans was a matter of necessity before a common enemy, but this did not prevent national concerns from taking over when the Assyrians were not threatening. Thus, the biblical representation of Ahab as fighting the Aramaeans toward the end of his reign is correct, according to several interpreters.

It should be noted, however, that Assyria was in a continual struggle with Hadadezer's coalition from his 6th year until at least the 14th year. Ahab is unlikely to have left the coalition during this time; it is only in the 18th year that a new king of Israel is mentioned, and the coalition under Hadadezer is defeated. If Ahab fought the Aramaeans, it would have been early in his reign, not in the last few years when he was part of the coalition organized by Hadadezer. It was only when Ahab was out of the way that the coalition was defeated.

Yet an explanation of the biblical picture that has become widely accepted in scholarship suggests the following: 1 Kings 20–22 contains material from the later Jehu dynasty (e.g. 2 Kgs 13), which has been mistakenly assigned to the reign of Ahab. In other words, the stories making Ahab fight the Aramaeans might have been transferred from the later Jehu dynasty (long after Ahab's death) when Israel was indeed weak in relation to the Aramaeans (Miller 1966, 1967, 1968; see also Pitard 1987, 114-25; Kuan 1995, 36-39).

Another issue concerns the relationship of Omri's kingdom with Moab. According to 2 Kings (1.1; 3.4-5) Moab was under the dominion of Israel but managed to break free after Ahab's death. No suggestion is made in the biblical text as to who subjugated Moab in the first place. The Mesha Stela states that Omri 'oppressed' Moab for his lifetime and half the lifetime of his son, 40 years, before Mesha threw off the Israelite yoke. There is a remarkable coincidence between the biblical and the extra-biblical data, as was noticed when the Moabite stone was first discovered (see the discussion under 'Omri' above). However, there are some discrepancies that either cannot be reconciled or at least call for an explanation.

One particular problem is the dating of Moab's vassalage to Israel. A period of 40 years is mentioned in the Mesha Stella inscription, obviously a round number. Omri is associated with the conquest of Moab; however, it is rather curious that Ahab is not mentioned at all, though the expression 'his son' might have been taken as a derogatory reference by not actually naming Ahab. It is interesting that the length of reigns of Omri and Ahab together total 34 years according to the biblical text (1 Kgs 16.23, 29), not far from forty years. It may be that the reigns of Omri and Ahab have been telescoped—after all, the Moabite scribe was making a general point, not giving a blow-by-blow historical narrative—and 'half the reign of his son' could be a reference to Jehoram (Ahab's son and Omri's grandson) rather than Ahab ('son' being used generically for a more remote descendent, 'grandson' in this case). Moab rebelled in the reign of Jehoram according to 1 Kgs 1.1. Jehoram reigned 12 years, and if we add 6 of these to the 34 of Omri and Ahab, we have 40. This fits both the biblical data and the information from the Mesha Stela.

One of the areas of difficulty often discussed is the number of chariots possessed by Ahab, according to the Assyrian texts. The text clearly reads '2000 chariots' (2 lim GIŠ.GIGIR.MEŠ), so the problems of trying to read a damaged text do not apply here. Yet the text is often emended, purely by conjecture since there is no question about the reading of the text as it stands. For example, Donald Wiseman's translation in 1958 reads '200 chariots' without so much as a footnote or comment to indicate that the text has been emended (1958, 47). Two points need to be made: the first is that the resources needed to maintain a large force of horses is not the precise equivalent of the economic support needed for manufacturing and supplying a modern tank regiment. 2000 chariots would need a large herd of horses, but these would not necessarily have been kept permanently in stalls. Grassland unsuitable for crops could still provide good grazing for horses kept in reserve until a national emergency arose.

A second point is that this force may not have been supplied by the kingdom of Israel alone (Kuan 1995, 39-47). 1 Kings 22.4 suggests that Judah was subordinate to Israel, perhaps being a vassal (cf. Knauf 2007), as was Moab. Also, Tyre and Sidon are not mentioned in Shalmaneser's inscription, either as opposing his advance or as paying tribute. However, if they were allies of Israel (as indeed they are so presented by the biblical text), they would be neither paying tribute to Assyria nor listed separately in the inscription.

Another famous incident is that of Naboth's vineyard, but there are good reasons for thinking this story actually originated in the Persian period and is only a subsequent insertion into the Ahab story (Rofé 1988). With regard to the Elijah and Elisha stories that form a part of the Ahab and sons story, see below (pp. 56-57).

Jehoshaphat (1 Kings 22)

The reign of Asa's son Jehoshaphat is summarized in 1 Kgs 22.41-47. He is labelled as righteous by the biblical writer, though it is admitted that the high places continued to function. Of course they did, because the concept of centralized worship apparently arose only much later (see Chapter 6, pp. 86-90 below). The other point made is that he was a great warrior (1 Kgs 22.46). Earlier in the chapter, he is supposed to have supported Ahab in one of his battles (exactly what this battle was is problematic), which supports his reputation as a military leader, but we have no references to him outside the biblical text.

Jehoshaphat's treatment in 1 Kings is surprisingly brief. It is in the book of 2 Chronicles that we have an extensive discussion of his reign. The long additional section in 2 Chronicles 17, 19, and 20.1-30 has Jehoshaphat ruling a magnificent kingdom in which the Torah is taught, the nations round about send gifts, a formidable military force is organized, and a great coalition of Moab, Ammon, and Seir is defeated. In light of our downgrading of Solomon's grandiose kingdom (Chapter 3) to something less impressive than the biblical text, the description of Jehoshaphat's Judah according to 2 Chronicles seems rather unlikely. It exemplifies the way in which the Chronicler has enhanced the theological picture compared to Kings.

Ahaziah and Jehoram of Israel and Joram and Ahaziah of Judah (1 Kings 22.52 to 2 Kings 9.29)

We actually have little information on the kings themselves (confined to 1 Kgs 22.52-54; 2 Kgs 3.1-3; 8.16-29; 9.15-29). The text gives priority to the story of Elisha the prophet, which complicates the narrative. Whereas a historian's interest is primarily on the political developments, the biblical writer was most impressed by the theological aspect of Elisha and his supposed activities. Basically all the text says about Ahaziah son of Ahab (who ruled only two years) is that he was wicked. The 12 years of his brother Jehoram are also dismissed as wicked, except that he removed the 'pillars of Baal' set up by Ahab (2 Kgs 3.2). The circumstances and significance of this are not presented to the reader.

The next king of Judah was Joram son of Jehoshaphat. Joram was said to be wicked and to have married Athaliah, sister of Ahab (2 Kgs 8.26, though 8.18 seems—mistakenly—to identify her as a daughter of Ahab). Also, under him Edom rebelled and broke away from Judahite rule (2 Kgs 8.20-22), according to the text. His son Ahaziah (whose uncle was Ahab of Israel) was king of Judah after Joram. He allied with Jehoram of Israel and both fought against Hazael king of the Aramaeans. Jehoram was wounded and went to Jezreel to recover. While Amaziah was visiting him there, Jehu rebelled and killed both Jehoram king of Israel and Amaziah king of Judah at the same time (2 Kgs 9.16-28).

An extra-biblical source that may tell us something about these events is the Tel Dan Inscription. The following is my reading of the first fragment found in 1993 (Biran and Naveh 1993) with a minimum of reconstruction:

>] my father went up [
> my father lay down (died?). He went to [Is-]
> rael earlier in the land. My father [(or "in the land of my father")
> I—Hadad went before me [
> x my king. And I killed of [them char-]
> ot and thousands (or 2000) of riders [
> king of Israel. And I kill[ed
> xx 'house of David' (*bytdwd*). And I set [
> xx the land. They x[
> another, and xxxx [ki-
> ng over Is[rael
> siege over [

The second fragment (actually two fragments that fit together) does not clearly join onto the first, and the reconstruction based on putting the two together strikes me as purely speculative (cf. Athas 2003, 175-91). I read the second fragment as follows, with little hypothetical reconstruction:

>] and cut [
>] battle/fought against xx [
>]x and went up the king x [
>] and Hadad made king [
>] I went up from Sheva'/seven [
> seven]ty tied/harnessed x[
> Jeho]ram son [
> Ahaz]yahu son [

This inscription has been subject to a number of interpretations, some of which are quite compelling, but they rely generally on the recon-struction of the original editors. However, it does seem to me that in the last two lines above the restoration of 'J(eh)oram' is virtually certain, and of 'Ahaziah' quite reasonable. If so, this favours assigning the inscription to Hazael and the interpretations that follow from it. Basing himself on the Tel Dan Inscription Lipiński (2000, 373-80), for example, has recently argued that Jehoram and Ahaziah were slain by Hazael, not Jehu. This interpretation has become fairly widely accepted. Can it be reconciled with the biblical text which has the two kings slain by Jehu? This is not difficult, since Hazael would have considered the actions of Jehu, who was his vassal, as his own actions. It was not an uncommon practice in royal inscriptions for the ruler to claim for himself the actions of his subordinates. But we cannot be certain that the picture of the biblical text is actually what happened, either, and the reconstruction of the Tell Dan inscription is of course not as certain as some seem to suggest.

Elijah and Elisha and the Prophetic Narrative Cycle

As discussed above (p. 20) the prophetic narrative is an important feature in the books of Kings. The presence of Elijah as a central figure in the Ahab story, and of him and his successor Elisha in the stories of the successors to Ahab, draws attention to this important element of the prophetic legends within 1 and 2 Kings. Although our concern in the present chapters of this book is the history question, we still have to consider what the stories about prophets tell us about the history of the time, especially since the Elijah and Elisha stories take up a good deal of the reigns of the Omride kings. Some of these prophetic stories may be 'pre-Deuteronomic', that is, they were in existence before the Deuteronomist edited the narrative of 1 and 2 Kings.

Thus, Anthony Campbell (1986) has argued that at the core of 1 Samuel 1 to 1 Kings 1 is a 'Prophetic Record' that goes back as early as the ninth century. Campbell's argument for the ninth century looks prima facie reasonable, but so does the more conventional date in the seventh century. Certainly, this optimism for early narratives in 1 and 2 Samuel has not been widely matched, since evidence of late composition, editing, and insertion is usually found. For example, Thomas C. Römer (2005, 144-45) notes that the Ark Narrative does not contain Deuteronomistic language, but rather than its being early (or pre-Deuteronomistic), it might well be *post*-Deuteronomistic.

Our concern is not with the books of Samuel but the books of Kings, but the problem is essentially the same, since there are many prophetic stories in 1 and 2 Kings, and at least some of them form a story cycle. Yet many of the prophetic stories are late. For example, as we have it the story in 1 Kings 13 (about a prophecy against Jeroboam) comes from a time at least 300 years later than Jeroboam, because of the reference to Josiah (1 Kgs 13.2). This is followed directly by another prophetic story, which has to do with the illness and subsequent death of Jeroboam's son and the prophecy of Ahijah that Jeroboam's family will be wiped out (1 Kgs 14.1-18).

The Elijah story makes him primarily an opponent of Baal. This might well be a correct memory, since there is likely to have been a 'Yhwh-alone party' (as argued by Morton Smith 1971), alongside the normally polytheistic society of Israel at the time. If Elijah opposed Baal worship and even had Baal cult functionaries slaughtered, it is hardly any wonder that he attracted the wrath of Jezebel, since he was attacking her national god (on Jezebel and religion, see Chapter 6, pp. 86-90). The miracle stories, including his being taken up to heaven, are what we expect to find in such prophetic legends and are not of interest from a historical point of view (though they may tell something about the phenomenon of prophecy in Israel).

As with Elijah, the Elisha story may contain genuine remembrances of a prophet who was leader of a prophetic community but who occasionally interacted even with the royal court. Yet many of the details are nothing less than miraculous and excluded from the realm of history. Certain religious figures gather stories around themselves that include the performance of miracles and other supernatural acts. This process of embellishing the stories of 'holy men' with wondrous deeds is known through history. In some cases, these stories simply confirm the importance of the prophetic figure to the community which remembered him and preserved his memory and story. These tell us about prophecy but not much about history. Yet since kings at the time did consult prophetic and mantic figures, the details of the Elijah and Elisha stories that relate to kings like Ahab may have a foundation in the history of the king in question, though making historical judgments about what actually took place is often very difficult.

Jehu (2 Kings 9–10)

With Jehu we once again have an Israelite ruler who is mentioned by the Assyrians.

According to the text of 2 Kings, Jehu began his reign with a blood bath: he first slaughtered the kings of both Israel and Judah, then Jezebel the queen mother; he then had 70 sons of Ahab executed by their guardians, relatives of Ahaziah slaughtered, and the other members of the house of Ahab killed. Immediately afterward, he had all the Baal worshippers assembled at the temple of Baal in Samaria and proceeded to butcher them. In spite of this zeal, which Yhwh supposedly commended, Jehu still followed in the ways of Jeroboam, and Hazael of Damascus began to take away territory, including the areas of Gilead and Bashan, northeast of the Sea of Galilee.

Jehu's slaying of Jezebel is a curious incident. Since the Ahab story had painted her as completely wicked, it is hardly surprising that Jehu had her put to death. But as already noted, her story is that of a foreign princess brought to Samaria as Ahab's wife and queen. She naturally brought her own cult, and her husband had a temple to Baal constructed for her. The biblical text claims that she persecuted the prophets of Yhwh (e.g. 1 Kgs 18.4), but religious persecution was not normally the actions of a polytheist; furthermore, as noted above (pp. 50-51), Ahab was himself a worshipper of Yhwh, and consulted prophets of Yhwh about the future (1 Kgs 22.6). The children that he and Jezebel produced had Yhwh names (1 Kgs 22.40; 2 Kgs 1.17; 3.1).

It seems that Jezebel's persecutions took place only in reaction to Elijah's attack on the Baal cult personnel: if he had her Baal prophets killed, it is hardly surprising that she sought his life! Similarly, when Jehu came for her, she made herself up, as a queen would, and met him with regal defiance, even though she knew she was about to die. According to the most recent studies by Dagmar Pruin (2006, 2007), only a couple of the traditions go back close to the original events: the revolt of Jehu and the fragment of Elijah as a rainmaker. Other parts of the tradition seem to be later, such as Naboth's vineyard, Jezebel's power and independence, and the image of Elijah as a champion of Yhwh worship, with Jezebel and her 450 prophets of Baal and 400 prophets of Asherah as his chief opponent.

One will notice that the concern of the text is, once again, the Aramaeans. Nothing is said about the Assyrians, yet it was the Assyrians who made Jehu a tributary. Shalmaneser III (who had fought Ahab) took tribute from him, and he appears to be bowing to the Assyrian king on the Black Obelisk, which has the inscription: 'At that time I received the tribute of the Tyrians, the Sidonians, and Jehu of Bit-Ḫumri [Israel]' (Grayson 1996, 60 [A.0.102.12: 21-30]). Much has been made by some writers about the designation of Jehu as 'son of Omri', as some translations render the final phrase. One explanation is that the writer of the inscription did not know that Jehu was not a son of Omri but a ursurper to the throne. However, the other inscriptions of Shalmaneser show that the ideogram rendered DUMU, 'son of', is used in a number of cases simply to designate a citizen of a particular country (hence, the translation 'man of'), though the person so designated usually happens to be the king. See the designation of Adramu king of Hamath as DUMU *A-gu-ú-si*, Aḫunu king of Adini as DUMU *A-di-ni*, and Ḫaiiānu king of Gabbari as DUMU *Gab-ba-ri* in the Kurkh Monolith (Grayson 1996, 17-18 [A.0.102.2: 15, 24, 27]) (also the discussion in Tadmor 1973, 149; Kuan 1995, 52-53 n. 167). Thus, I would argue that 'son of Omri' simply means 'king of Bit-Humri (Israel)'.

Once the coalition assembled by Hadadezer had broken up, Hazael alone stood against the Assyrians. Jehu, along with other small kingdoms of the region, submitted to the Assyrians and paid tribute. Campaigns against Hazael are mentioned for Shalmaneser III's 18th (841 BCE) and 21st years (838 BCE). After that the Assyrians ceased to march into the western part of their empire for several decades, leaving Damascus to dominate the region. The picture of Hazael and his son Bar-Hadad (called Ben-Hadad in the biblical text) as causing trouble for Israel is a realistic one (2 Kgs 10.32-33; 12.18-19; 13.3-6; see further p. 60 below).

Athaliah and Joash of Judah (2 Kings 11–12)

The account of Athaliah's attempted coup and the temple repair under Joash would not have come from a chronicle. Both involve priests and the temple, but whether they were based on oral tradition or a written source is unknown.

As the daughter of Omri (or possibly Ahab), Athialiah had been married to Jehoram son of Jehoshaphat king of Judah (2 Kgs 8.18, 26). She was the mother to Jehoram's son Ahaziah (who was assassinated by Jehu), and she seized the throne of Judah after Ahaziah's death (2 Kgs 11.1-3). Jehoram's young son Joash was hidden away, however, to prevent his being killed by Athaliah, according to the text. After the passage of several years, the high priest Jehoiada arranged to have Joash crowned king, at which point Athaliah was herself taken out and executed. Whether things happened exactly as the text suggests is a question, but the basic scenario looks credible: such attempted coups and rivalry over the throne are widely attested in history.

The main episode related about Joash is that he ordered money to be collected and used to repair the temple (2 Kgs 12). After his coronation, the high priest supposedly had a temple to Baal torn down and its priest slain (2 Kgs 11.18). Although this might be possible, one must ask, when was this temple to Baal built and who by? One suspects a literary creation in which Jehu's destruction of the temple for Baal in Samaria has been duplicated here. Joash is said to be a righteous king: Is he righteous because of the deeds recounted, or are the deeds created because he had a reputation of being righteous? Two episodes could have come from a court chronicle: the first is the attack of the Aramaean king Hazael (2 Kgs 12.18-19: this fits the archaeology of Gath [Maeir and Uziel 2007, 31-35]); the other is that Joash was assassinated in a conspiracy (2 Kgs 12.21-22).

Jehoahaz and Jehoash of Israel (2 Kings 13)

The next two kings of Israel were part of the Jehu dynasty. First was Jehu's son Jehoahaz under whom Israel was harassed and its territory diminished by Hazael the Aramaean (2 Kgs 13.1-9). It is the small size of his army and other details that make some scholars think that some material in the Ahab cycle actually belongs to Jehoahaz but was taken over (accident or design) into the Ahab account (see p. 52 above). He was followed by his son Jehoash about whom we know little that is likely to have come from a chronicle. We have only the Elisha prophetic legend that says Jehoash could have destroyed Aramaean oppression if he had only read Elisha's mind and extended his symbolic act! The one item that could have come from a chronicle is that once Hazael died, Jehoash began to recover some towns under his successor Ben-Hadad (Bar-Hadad) that had been taken from Israel by Hazael (2 Kgs 13.25). The reason for this recovery is not given by the biblical text (which only relates it to the actions of Elisha), but the Assyrian records help us out. After many decades during which the Assyrians did not come to the Mediterranean, they once again intervened in the west under Adad-nirari III (ca. 806–796).

We know that a coalition of small states, including Bar-Hadad son of Hazael, attacked Zakkur of Hamath (Zakkur Inscription [quoted in Grabbe 2007b, 130]) and apparently went on to challenge the Assyrians. Not only does the biblical text have the sequence Hazael, followed by Bar-Hadad (Hebrew Ben-Hadad), but the 'saviour' of 2 Kgs 13.5 is probably a reference to the Assyrian help. The Zakkur Inscription probably alludes to this same anti-Assyrian coalition, whereas Zakkur is pro-Assyrian and seems to have been delivered by Assyrian intervention. The Joash of Israel who is being relieved of the oppression from Bar-Hadad is mentioned in the el-Rimah Assyrian inscription (Grayson 1996, 211 [A.0.104.7.4-8]) as paying tribute to the Assyrians. Finally, the fall of Damascus about 802 (for the possible dates, see Kuan 1995, 93-106), as described in the el-Rimah and other inscriptions, would have taken the pressure off Israel and others who were under the yoke of Damascus. About 780–775 BCE Shamshi-ilu the Assyrian commander for the region collected tribute from Ḥadiiāni of Damascus. This would suggest that Damascus was not able to do just anything it wished. Thus, although the biblical text cannot be confirmed in detail, the general picture given fits the situation in the last part of the ninth century and beginning of the eighth, as we know it from extra-biblical sources.

Amaziah and Azariah (Uzziah) of Judah
(2 Kings 14.1-22; 15.1-7)

Amaziah is supposed to have been righteous like his father Joash (though the high places were admittedly not removed, which is what we would expect at this time). Unsurprisingly, he executed those who had assassinated his father. He supposedly defeated the Edomites and captured Sela. But when he challenged Jehoash of Israel to battle, Amaziah was soundly defeated, captured, had to pay tribute and send hostages, and have part of the wall of Jerusalem destroyed. Like his father, he was slain in a conspiracy (though he fled to Lachish, trying to escape). All of this is plausible, but none of it can be confirmed. Unfortunately, there are still some major disputes about interpreting the archaeology of Edom that might otherwise help us here (see Grabbe 2007b, 93-98).

Amaziah was succeeded by Azariah (called Uzziah in 2 Chronicles 26). Once again he is supposed to have been righteous, even though he did not remove the high places. In other words, he followed the normal religious expectations of his own time rather than the later judgment of the Deuteronomists (see Chapter 6, pp. 86-90 below). His reward was to be stricken with leprosy, and his son Jotham became co-ruler. (Although co-rulership is often postulated in order to overcome chronological problems, this is one of the few actually attested in the text.)

2 Chronicles 26.5-20 is a curious text that gives all sorts of information not in the text of Kings: Uzziah is supposed to have made various conquests against the Philistines, Arabs, and Ammonites, to have built major fortifications and expanded the military, and to have extended cultivation and prosperity. But then in a state of hubris, he tried to offer incense in the temple, against the protests of the priests, and was struck with leprosy—even though David and Solomon had offered sacrifices, as was normal for Judahite kings at this time. The Chronicler's version seems to be the product of a vivid imagination.

Jeroboam (II) of Israel (2 Kings 14.23-29)

Once again the biblical text makes light of an Israelite king that other sources indicate was a significant ruler. The main judgment of the text is that he was wicked, yet it knows that he restored the northern part of Israel at the expense of the Aramaeans: 2 Kgs 14.26-27 is almost apologetic that this recovery was allowed to happen! The exact territory recovered is unclear since the portion of the text that might have come from a chronicle (2 Kgs 14.28) seems to be in disorder; the suggestion is that much of Syria was taken, but this is unlikely. The important historical point, though, is that Jeroboam II reversed the ascendancy of Damascus over Israel; however, it should be noted that the reason is primarily that Assyria had returned to the west and was putting unstoppable pressure on the Aramaeans (cf. Grayson 1996, 211 [A.0.104.7: 4-8]; *ANET*, 281-82). Jeroboam took advantage of the Assyrian attack to open another front against Bar-Hadad ruler of Damascus.

Zechariah, Shallum, and Menahem of Israel
(2 Kings 15.8-22)

Jeroboam's son Zechariah lasted only six months before being assassinated in a conspiracy by Shallum, but the latter was then killed only a month later by Menahem. The text says that Zechariah was wicked, though exactly how he accomplished this wickedness in a reign of half a year is not stated. Strangely, no such condemnation is made of Shallum, though this was probably an oversight on the part of the Deuteronomist.

Menahem began his rule not only with executing Shallum but then attacking Tiphsah and committing an atrocity against the inhabitants for not submitting. But the main event was that Tiglath-pileser III (here called Pul) of Assyria came against Israel and required a tribute of a thousand silver talents. Menahem raised the funds by requiring 50 shekels from all the 'men of substance' in the kingdom. Since there are usually 3,000 shekels in a talent, this suggests 60,000 'men of substance', whatever the phrase means exactly. This sounds exaggerated, but did all the tribute come from their contribution? Are these figures even accurate? Tiglath-pileser's tribute list in the Calah Annals lists Menahem of Samaria as one who paid tribute to him (Tadmor 1994, 69-71), though the amount is not given.

Jotham and Ahaz of Judah (2 Kings 15.32–16.20)

Uzziah's son Jotham is said to have been righteous, even though the high places remained in place; once again the reason for this judgment of being good is unclear. Apart from some renovations to the temple, the main claim to fame of his reign (as mentioned by the text) is that Rezin (Aramaic Raḍyan; see next section) of Damascus and Pekah of Israel began an assault on Judah.

The main attack on Judah came under Jotham's son Ahaz, however, according to both 2 Kgs 16.5-9 and Isaiah 7. They did not succeed in overcoming Israel because Ahaz sent a bribe to Tiglath-pileser III (that is, he made himself a vassal of Assyria, which meant that he was now required to pay an annual tribute) who attacked Damascus and killed Rezin. This invasion of Aram and death of Rezin is described in Tigath-pileser's Summary Inscription 4 (Tadmor 1994, 138-41); the Assyrian king also removed Pekah from being king over Samaria and replaced him with Hoshea (for more details, see the next section). The main part of the account is about Ahaz's supposed religious apostasy in building another altar in the temple, alongside the original.

Last Kings of Israel and Fall of Samaria
(2 Kings 15.23-31; 17)

Menahem's son was Pekahiah; the only datum in the text is that his two-year reign was another example of wickedness. He was assassinated by his aide Pekah who seized the throne. At some point, Pekah apparently allied with Rezin the Aramaean (discussed in previous section). Rezin (his name was the Aramaic *Raḍyan*, which his name in the Akkadian inscriptions apparently reflects). Although the 'Syro-Ephraimite war' (2 Kgs 15.29; 16.5-9; Isa. 7) is not described as such in the Assyrian annals, it is compatible with everything so far known. In the end, though, both Rezin and his alleged ally Pekah lost out. Tiglath-pileser III took Damascus about 732 BCE and exiled many of the Aramaeans (Tadmor 1994, 138 [Summary Inscription 4, 7'-8'], 186 [Summary Inscription 9, reverse 3-4]).

As indicated, we have a good deal of extra-biblical material in the Assyrian inscriptions, which allows us to test the historicity of the biblical account. Summary Inscription 4 tells about how Tiglath-pileser had Pekah removed for disloyalty and replaced by Hoshea (Tadmor 1994, 140 [Summary Inscription 4, 15'-19'], 188 [Summary Inscription 9, 9-11]). This is remarkably close to 2 Kgs 15.30. Perhaps the one discrepancy is whether Tiglath-pileser or Hoshea deposed Pekah, but this is probably a matter of wording. The removal of Pekah is not likely to have happened without Tiglath-pileser's ultimate say-so, and one suspects that Hoshea acted only when he knew that he had Assyrian backing.

The Mesopotamian sources also fill in a great deal about the siege and capture of Samaria and deportation of many Israelites, but they also raise a number of questions. In particular, what part did Shalmaneser V play and what hand did Sargon II have in the matter? Sargon II claims to have conquered Samaria, and some scholars have accepted these claims; however, the account in 2 Kgs 17.3-6 that this siege and capture of the city took place in the time of Shalmaneser V is supported by the

Babylonian Chronicle 1 (i 27-31). The argument that the various sources can be reconciled is probably correct, though more than one solution is possible. Bob Becking argued that there were two conquests of Samaria, one by Shalmaneser V in 723 BCE and another by Sargon II in 720 BCE in response to a rebellion of Ilu-bi'di of Hamath (1992, 2002).

It seems likely that both Shalmanese V and Sargon II were in some way involved in the end of Samaria. Yet there is no evidence in the archaeology that the city was destroyed. Perhaps the biblical text does not clearly envisage a destruction of the city, but the archaeological evidence also seems to be against a wholesale deportation of the population (though a small portion does seem to have been removed and replaced by outside settlers (Zertal 1989). As to the question of whether the Israelites were really taken to the places alleged in 2 Kgs 17.6 and of whether peoples from the places listed in 2 Kgs 17.24 were actually brought in, there is now some evidence that some movement of populations between the two regions actually took place (Becking 1992, 61-104; 2002; Na'aman and Zadok 2000; Oded 1979, 69-71; 2000, 91-99; Cogan and Tadmor 1988, 197, 209-10). But whether the extent of the deportation was as great as described in the biblical text is definitely to be queried.

Summary and Conclusions

This chapter has looked at the material stretching from 1 Kings 16 to 2 Kings 17. It is in this section that we start to have considerable extra-biblical parallels. There are many statements that are supported by these extra-biblical sources or that at least have a prima facie probability, even if there is no external support. Yet if we look carefully at the material of this text, we see few passages of any length that seem to be staightforward narratives. On the contrary, the whole section is dominated by prophetic stories or theological interests. For example, an entire chapter is devoted to the reign of Joash of Judah (2 Kgs 12), yet most of the space concerns how money was collected for the repair of the house of Yhwh. Whereas the reign of Omri is described succinctly and with the surface appearance of factuality, the reign of Ahab is dominated by stories about the prophets Elijah and Elisha. Indeed, there is little from 1 Kings 17 to 2 Kings 9—a large part of this section of text—that does not relate to Elijah and Elisha. Much of this long section of 15 chapters is a series of prophetic stories and anecdotes. Some of these relate to national events, but a good deal is purely focused on the doings of the prophet.

In some instances, we evidently have material from a court chronicle or the like (though it may be taken from a summary of such a chronicle rather than directly excerpted from the chronicle itself). But the quality of the material is made clearer in many cases when it is contrasted with the parallel account in 2 Chronicles. Where the latter has a more extensive account, it is obvious most of the time that it did not have additional sources or—if so—that they were not of the same quality as those in the books of Kings. Thus, the narrative in the books of Kings has useful data for reconstructing the history of Israel and Judah, if it is used carefully and critically.

Chapter 5

THE BOOKS OF KINGS AND HISTORY: FROM THE FALL OF SAMARIA TO THE FALL OF JERUSALEM

Outline of 2 Kings 18–25

Here is an outline of the contents (for a form critical outline, see Long 1991, 190-290). Parallels from 2 Chronicles are also listed (where Kings or Chronicles omits material found in the other, a dash [—] is given to show the lack of material).

18–20 (//2 Chr. 29–32): reign of Hezekiah.
   18.1-8 (2 Chr. 29.1-2): summary of Hezekiah's reign.
     18.7-8 (//2 Chr. —): rebelled against Assyria; struck Philistines as far as Gaza.
   18.9-12 (//2 Chr. —): Shalmaneser besieges Samaria; deports the Israelites.
   — (//2 Chr. 29.3–31.21): Hezekiah cleanses temple; renews service; provides for priests and Levites; celebrates Passover.
   18.13-16 (//2 Chr. 32.1): Sennacherib attacks towns of Judah; Hezekiah capitulates and pays tribute.
   — (//2 Chr. 32.2-8): Hezekiah prepares for a siege by Assyrians.
   18.17-37 (//2 Chr. 32.9-19): Sennacherib sends Rabshakeh and other officials to speak to Hezekiah's men.
   19.1-7 (//2 Chr. 32.20): Hezekiah mourns and calls for Isaiah.
     19.5-7 (//2 Chr. —): Isaiah's message to Hezekiah.
   19.8-13 (//2 Chr. —): Sennacherib attacked by Tirhakah; sends letter to Hezekiah.
   19.14-34 (//2 Chr. —): Hezekiah presents Sennacherib's letter to Yhwh.
     19.14-19: Hezekiah's prayer.
     19.20-34: Isaiah's message to Hezekiah from Yhwh.
   19.35-37 (//2 Chr. 32.21-23): Sennacherib's army destroyed; returns to Nineveh; assassinated.
   20.1-11 (//2 Chr. 32.24-26): Hezekiah's illness.
     20.1-3: Isaiah's message that he would die.
     20.4-7: Yhwh answers Hezekiah's prayer and heals him.
     20.8-11: sign of shadow receding 10 steps on sundial.
   20.12-19 (//2 Chr. 32.27-31): embassy of Merodach-baladan of Babylon.

20.13: Hezekiah shows off his wealth.

20.14-19: conversation between Hezekiah and Isaiah.

  20.16-18: Isaiah's prophecy against Hezekiah.

20.20-21 (//2 Chr. 32.32-33): summary of Hezekiah's reign; his death; Manasseh takes throne.

21.1-18 (//2 Chr. 33.1-20): reign of Manasseh.

21.1-9 (//2 Chr. 33.1-9): summary of Manasseh's reign, emphasizing the evils.

— (//2 Chr. 33.10-13): Manasseh taken captive to Babylon; repents; turns to Yhwh.

— (//2 Chr. 33.14-17): Manasseh builds Jerusalem's wall; removes religious abominations.

21.10-15 (//2 Chr. —): Yhwh speaks against Manasseh through prophets.

21.16 (//2 Chr. —): Manasseh puts innocent to death; fills Jerusalem with blood.

21.17 (//2 Chr. 33.18): other events in annals of the kings of Judah.

— (//2 Chr. 33.19): words of Hozai recording Manasseh's sins and his prayer of repentance.

21.18 (//2 Chr. 33.20): Manasseh dies and is buried.

21.19-26 (//2 Chr. 33.21-25): reign of Amon.

21.19 (//2 Chr. 33.21): begins reign at age 22 and reigns 2 years.

21.20-22 (//2 Chr. 33.22-23): wicked like his father.

21.23-26 (//2 Chr. 33.24-25): assassinated in a conspiracy.

22.1–23.30 (//2 Chr. 34.1–35.27): reign of Josiah.

22.1-2 (//2 Chr. 34.1-2): initial summary of reign.

— (//2 Chr. 34.3-7): begins purge of shrines and cults in his 12th year.

22.3-7 (//2 Chr. 34.8-13): Josiah orders the cleansing of the temple in his 18th year.

22.8-10 (//2 Chr. 34.14-18): finding of scroll and reading of it to Josiah.

22.11-20 (//2 Chr. 34.19-28): prophetess Huldah consulted about the scroll.

23.1-3 (//2 Chr. 34.29-32): covenant with the people to keep the laws of the scroll.

23.4-14 (//2 Chr. —): temple cleansed; priests of high places brought to Jerusalem; other cults and objects removed.

23.15-18 (//2 Chr. —): Bethel purified; destruction of Jeroboam's altar.

23.19-20 (//2 Chr. —): rest of Samaria purified of cult places and priests.

— (//2 Chr. 34.33): summary of Josiah's reign.

23.21-23 (//2 Chr. 35.1-19): Passover kept.

23.24 (//2 Chr. —): divination eliminated.

23.25-27 (//2 Chr. —): prophecy of Judah's destruction postponed because of Josiah' righteousness.

23.28-30 (//2 Chr. 35.20-27): Josiah's death at the hands of Necho.

23.30-34 (//2 Chr. 36.1-4): reign of Jehoahaz.

23.31-32 (//2 Chr. 36.2): summary of reign.

23.33-34 (//2 Chr. 36.3): removed by Necho; taken to Egypt; tribute imposed.

23.34–24.7 (//2 Chr. 36.4-8): reign of Jehoiakim.

23.35 (//2 Chr. —): Jehoiakim collects money for tribute.

23.36-37 (//2 Chr. 36.5): summary of reign.

24.1-7 (//2 Chr. 36.6-8): vassal of Nebuchadnezzar 3 years, then rebels; raids against Judah by Chaldeans, et al.; dies.

— (//2 Chr. 36.6-7: Jehoiakim taken to Babylon, with temple vessels.)

24.8-16 (//2 Chr. 36.8-10): reign of Jehoiachin.
  24.8-9 (//2 Chr. 36.9): summary of reign.
  24.10-16 (//2 Chr. 36.10): Nebuchadnezzar takes city; deports Jehoiachin and
                               family and others to Babylon.
24.17–25.21 (//2 Chr. 36.10-21): reign of Zedekiah.
  24.18-20 (//2 Chr. 36.11-12): summary of reign.
  25.1-21 //2 Chr. 36.13-21): Zedekiah rebels; Jerusalem taken by
                               Nebuchadnezzar; king and people exiled.
25.22-30 (//2 Chr. —): aftermath of fall of Jerusalem.
  25.22-26: brief governorship of Gedaliah; people flee to Egypt.
  25.27-30: Jehoiachin released from prison.

Reign of Hezekiah (2 Kings 18–20)

The reign of Hezekiah is an event about which we have a considerable amount of information, especially in the biblical text but also in the Assyrian records, especially relating to the invasion of Sennacherib in 701 BCE. Only an outline of the information and historical problems can be given here (see Grabbe 2007b, 195-200 for further information and references; see also the essays in Grabbe [ed.] 2003).

The account of Hezekiah's reign begins with a religious and cultic reform (2 Kgs 18.3-6). This reform has been widely accepted in scholarship (e.g. Albertz 1994, 1:180-86), but it is now also widely questioned (e.g. Na'aman 1995). The problem is that it looks very much like the reform later ascribed to Josiah. Did Josiah try to revive what failed under Hezekiah, or did the biblical writer borrow from Josiah's story to improve Hezekiah's piety by literary invention? In his more recent study, Na'aman (2002) looked at the abandonment of cult places as a result of alleged cult reforms, with special emphasis on Arad and Beersheba; he concluded that these represented an attempt to consolidate royal power.

The latest archaeological discussion by Zeev Herzog (2010) continues to argue that the cancelling of the temples at Arad and Beersheba supports the story of Hezekiah's reform. His is mainly a critique of Na'aman, claiming that the latter has completely misunderstood the archaeology. However, he does not really respond to Knauf's restructuring and redating of the archaeology that places the dismantling of the temples under Manasseh (see below). It should also be kept in mind that David Ussishkin (1988) redated the sanctuary to the seventh century and put the cancellation of it to the sixth century BCE, while L.S. Fried (2002) argued that the archaeology of the *bāmôt* does not support the alleged cult reforms of the text. Herzog made the curious statement:

The suggestion to interpret finds related to remains of cult at Arad and Tel Beer-sheba as evidence of cultic reform in general, and the reform of King Hezekiah in particular, has won the support of archaeologists and—at the same time—the sharp criticism mainly of Historians and Biblical scholars. (Herzog 2010, 179)

However, apart from the fact that there are archaeologists (already noted above) who do not agree with Herzog, it should not be overlooked that Herzog dismisses the event of a religious reform under Josiah, which seems even more radical than dismissing a reform under Hezekiah!

The analysis of the biblical narrative has been an important part of the discussion relating to historicity. On the invasion of Sennacherib, more than a century ago B. Stade (1886) produced a basic analysis that has continued to dominate the literary discussion. He noted that 18.14-16 had already been recognized as an insertion from good sources that was early. He then argued that 18.13, 17 to 19.9a was parallel to 19.9b-37. Neither of these narratives could be considered trustworthy historical sources but were both 'legendary', even if here and there they contained a correct historical datum. B. Childs (1967) refined Stade's analysis, with the following terms:

Account A: 2 Kgs 18.13-16.
Account B_1: 2 Kgs 18.17–19.9a, 36-37//Isa. 36.1–37.9a
Account B_2: 2 Kgs 19.9b-35//Isa. 37.9b-36

Attempts to rationalize the various narratives in the biblical text already began in the infancy of Assyriology, with the suggestion of two invasions of Sennacherib. The question continued to be debated until the present, with eminent scholars for more than one invasion and others against it (see the survey in Grabbe [ed.] 2003, 20-34). It was W.H. Shea (1985) who advanced well beyond contemporary positions with a lengthy circum-stantial argument that Sennacherib had conducted a second invasion after 689 BCE; however, Shea's argument was refuted point by point by Frank Yurco (1991).

So how reliable are the accounts in 2 Kings 18–20? Noth gave an inter-pretation that depended almost entirely on 2 Kgs 18.16-19 (along with the Assyrian inscriptions); the rest of the biblical account was essentially ignored (1960, 266-69). This was basically the consensus of the discussion by the European Seminar in Historical Methodology (Grabbe [ed.] 2003): Account A was the most widely accepted as reliable but Accounts B_1 and B_2 were thought to be much later and unreliable compositions. W.R. Gallagher's study (1999) 'most closely adheres' to the approach that uses all sources and assumes that they are largely reliable and comes to some quite conservative conclusions about it.

In an important study S. Parpola (1980) showed that the name of Sennacherib's assassin had been wrongly interpreted for many years. It should be read as Arda-Mulišši of which the biblical Adrammelech (2 Kgs 19.37) is a corrupt but recognizable form. A question is how to take the visit of Merodach-baladan (called 'Berodach-baladan' in 2 Kings) to Jerusalem. Because a king of Babylon, Marduk-apla-dan, actually existed, some have wanted to suggest that this is a plausible story: the Babylonian king, who was rebelling against the Assyrians, was seeking support and allies. This might seem to be a valid argument until one considers the distance that Judah lay from Babylon and the lack of any possibility of giving help. The story looks more like an explanation of why Jerusalem fell to the Babylonians.

The '14th year' (2 Kgs 18.13) has been a major difficulty since the Assyrian inscriptions showed that Sennacherib's invasion was in 701 BCE. According to 18.1 Hezekiah became king in Hoshea's 3rd year, while Samaria fell in Hezekiah's 4th year. If so, the events of 701 would have taken place about Hezekiah's 25th year, not the '14th'. J.A. Montgomery (1951, 483) emended to the '24th year', but he expressed the view that the synchronism with Hoshea's reign was an error. Several other solutions have been advanced in the past few decades. In 1994 Na'aman surveyed the arguments on both sides and proposed that, though not conclusive, the balance of evidence favoured taking the 14th year as correct and dating Hezekiah's reign ca. 715–686 (1994). B. Becking (1992, 2001, 2003) also addressed some of the questions of chronology. He has argued for the dating of the fall of Samaria to 723 BCE, a year earlier than the conventional 722. He accepts that the synchronism made by the DtrH editor between the reigns of Hoshea and Hezekiah (2 Kgs 18.9-10) is based on Judaean archives. This means that the 14th year of Hezekiah has to be either spring 715 to spring 714 or autumn 716 to autumn 715. At that time Sargon II dispatched an expedition to Palestine that was relatively peaceful.

With such a large number of scholarly opinions the current situation can be stated succinctly as follows (see further Grabbe 2007b, 190-200). The firmest datum we have at the end of the eighth century is the invasion of Sennacherib. It can be precisely calculated to 701 BCE. We have detailed descriptions in the Assyrian sources, including mention of local Palestinian rulers by name (e.g. Hezekiah), and the widespread destruction has left a distinct mark in the archaeological record. There is substantial agreement that reliable memory of this is found in 2 Kgs 18.13-16, and rather less reliable memory in various other parts of 2 Kings 18–20 (Grabbe [ed.] 2003). The 'two-invasion' hypothesis, although once widely accepted, looks now to be in tatters. The main extra-biblical support has collapsed. Although Sennacherib's reign is poorly documented after 689 BCE, there does not seem to be any room for another campaign to Palestine.

The Egyptian data are also crucial to the question: When did the Egyptian pharaoh Taharqa take the throne and what was his age in 701 BCE? Although still debated, the weight of opinion seems to be that Taharqa was capable of leading a military expedition against the Assyrians in 701 BCE. Whether he did or not is naturally still a matter of debate, but the reason for his mention in 2 Kgs 19.9 probably derives from his later image as the great Egyptian (Nubian) king who stood up to Assyria (Dion 1988). However, the chronology of Hezekiah's reign remains disputed, and the way in which Jerusalem avoided a siege is considerably debated. How much longer Hezekiah ruled after 701 and what events took place in his reign are not matters of agreement. For a continuation of the debate, see Grabbe ([ed.] 2003, especially 308-23). As for Hezekiah's cult reform, there is still considerable question whether such took place, though the story might reflect some sorts of events during Hezekiah's reign.

Reign of Manasseh (2 Kings 21.1-18)

The name of Manasseh is one of the most infamous in the biblical text. He is perhaps equalled—but not surpassed—only by Ahab and Jezebel. This suggests that the long reign ascribed to him is likely to be a firm part of the tradition and thus to have some basis in fact, because a long life was often thought to show that the person was right with God. What emerges from recent study, however, is the importance of the reign of Manasseh. Far from being a time of depravity and fear, many think it represents a remarkable recovery from the devastations of Sennacherib. It must have given many Judaeans a return to some sort of prosperity and hope for the future.

What the archaeology suggests is that Judah made a significant recovery from the disaster of 701 (Finkelstein 1994; Finkelstein and Silberman 2001, 264-74). The important agricultural region of the Shephelah remained sparsely populated, probably the larger part of it having been removed from Judahite control. Elsewhere, though, settlements were re-established in destroyed southern areas, possibly with even a population increase. Settlements were also pushed into the marginal desert areas to make use of all possible land for agricultural purposes. Although dating is not easy, the suggestion is that this happened under Manasseh's leadership. Manasseh seems to have been responsible for building a city wall (2 Chr. 33.15), which could be the one dating from the seventh century discovered on the eastern slope of Jerusalem's southeastern hill (L. Tatum 2003, 300). It has also been proposed by E.A. Knauf that Manasseh built some prestige projects, including the Siloam tunnel (Knauf 2001) and a palace at Ramat Raḥel (Knauf 2005, 170).

Manasseh's existence is well attested in the Assyrian inscriptions. He is named as an apparently loyal subject paying the required tribute to both Esarhaddon and Ashurbanipal (though it has been pointed out that Manasseh's tribute is smaller than that of his neighbours [Finkelstein and Silberman 2001, 265]). He also supplied military assistance for Ashurbanipal's attack on Egypt. In addition, there is some evidence of the part played by Judah in the economy of the Assyrian empire, a role that would have benefited the inhabitants of Judah. The territory of Judah formed a significant link in the caravan trade from Arabia, which the Assyrians would have controlled. The Idumaean plateau gained a significant population at this time, with the trade route leading through the valley of Beersheba and the southern coastal plain to Gaza. There are indications of contact with South Arabia, and the seventh-century forts at Qadesh-barnea and Haseva might have been built with the protection of this trade in mind. A major olive oil production centre existed at Tel Miqne (usually identified with ancient Ekron); however, the olives were not grown locally but would most likely have been imported from the Samarian and Judaean highlands.

As far as Manasseh's 'apostasy' is concerned, Finkelstein and Silberman (2001, 265) think that there was simply a return to popular religion by the people of the countryside after Hezekiah's failed cultic reform (assuming there was such a reform, which was doubted above). Others would argue that nothing innovative from a religious point of view happened under Manasseh; rather, he was just blamed for what had been the traditional religion among the people for many centuries. This does not, though, rule out foreign influence, such as from Assyro-Aramaic astral cults (see further in Chapter 6, pp. 86-90 below).

One of the most curious episodes related in the Bible is about Manasseh's deportation to and imprisonment in Babylon, followed by a return to Jerusalem and his throne and by repentance of his wicked deeds. This story is found in only one passage, significantly in Chronicles (2 Chr. 33.10-17), but not a hint is found in 2 Kgs 21.1-18. Furthermore, other biblical passages know nothing of Manasseh's repentance (Jer. 15.4; 2 Kgs 23.12; 2 Chr. 33.22). If Manasseh actually did all this, why would the Deuteronomist omit it? He was either ignorant of the information or he deliberately suppressed it. It is difficult to believe that if such an incident took place, he had no information, so we must assume that he knew of Manasseh's repentance but purposefully ignored it. Is this likely? Yes, perhaps if the idea of an act of repentance on Manasseh's part created problems with his underlying pattern of presentation, but this would be a serious reflection on the claim made by some that the Deuteronomist was writing history. In sum, though, the story of Manasseh's having been arrested and taken 'with hooks and bound in bronze fetters' to Babylon is unlikely.

Reign of Amon (2 Kings 21.19-26)

We have no data on him other than what is in the Bible. He is unlikely to have been invented. It was unusual for a king to be assassinated, and there is nothing about Amon to give this a literary significance. Thus, it is likely to have happened. However, the figures given for his age look suspect: although it is theoretically possible that he had a child at age 16, this seems highly improbable. Possibly the problem is with the age of Josiah (see next section), though in cases of the sudden death of a king a minor child might well take the throne.

Reign of Josiah (2 Kings 22.1–23.30)

Despite the importance given to him in the biblical tradition, Josiah is known only from the biblical text. Neither the surviving Babylonian nor Egyptian records contain any reference to him. We are left with archaeology and the biblical text with which to make sense of his reign, though the Egyptian material and the Babylonian Chronicles provide useful background and contextual information. Many past reconstructions have depended on the picture in 2 Chronicles, even those aspects which differ at significant points from those in 2 Kings.

One theory that has held considerable sway for a number of decades is that Josiah was attempting to create a 'greater Israel', perhaps on the model of the Davidic kingdom. There are many obvious parallels between Josiah and David, though one could put these down to literary creation rather than actual activity of the ruler. The 'righteousness' of both kings is the most obvious contact, but the conquest of territory is another that many scholars have managed to glean from the biblical material: the attempt to return to a 'greater Israel' and a recovery of former glory. It has been argued that, although Josiah's reform was indeed religious, the basis of it was economic (Claburn 1973).

Na'aman (1991, 33-41; 2005b, 210-17) has argued, however, that there was no political vacuum which gave Josiah room to try to found a new Davidic 'empire'. Rather, the declining Assyrian power in the west was matched by the growing power of Egypt; indeed, there may have been an orderly transfer of territorial control by mutual agreement (Na'aman 1991, 40). Miller and Hayes (1986, 383-90) had already argued that Josiah was an Egyptian vassal his entire reign. Na'aman has gone on to create a picture of Judah as a vassal state during the entirety of Josiah's reign, first under the Assyrians and then under the Egyptians. This gave only very limited scope for expansion of territory. There is some evidence of shifting the border as far north as Bethel. However, the expansion further north into the Galilee or west into the area of Philistia are unjustified from either archaeology or the text.

It was once conventional to accept Josiah's reform at face value, but the question is currently much debated (Albertz 1994, 198-201; 2005; Lohfink 1995; Davies 2005; Knauf 2005). We have no direct evidence outside the biblical text, which makes us at least ask whether it is an invention of the Deuteronomist. The alleged absence of any reference to this reform in Jeremiah has always been a major puzzle. Some have found allusions here and there, but one has to admit that they are surprisingly obscure. Considering Jeremiah's overall message and position, he should have embraced such a reform and made copious comments about it. Some have seen evidence in the material remains (e.g. Uehlinger 1995, 2005), but others have argued against it (e.g. Niehr 1995). The central passage is 2 Kings 22–23, however. It is widely agreed that this passage has been the subject of Deuteronomistic editing, leaving the question of how much might be Deuteronomistic invention. Christof Hardmeier (2005) and Christoph Uehlinger (2005) argue that at the heart of 2 Kings 22–23 is a simple list of reform measures affecting mainly Jerusalem and perhaps Bethel, to which the Deuteronomistic editors have added an extensive superstructure that makes the reform much more extensive in scope and geography than the original list. Uehlinger argues that the original list— but not the much-expanded present text—is supported by the archaeology and iconography.

A related issue is the statement in 2 Chr. 34.3-7 that Josiah began to purge the country of the various shrines and cults in his 12th year (i.e. at age 20). This does not accord with 2 Kgs 22.3-7, which has the reform follow the discovery of the law book in the temple. This is not an easy issue to address because the description in 2 Kings 22–23 is an idealized one: the only question is how idealized. This is perhaps why a significant opinion of scholarship has accepted the statement in 2 Chr. 34.3-7 that

Josiah began his reform six years before the finding of the law book. Yet as Na'aman (1991, 38), among others, has pointed out, the theological motives of the writer of Chronicles have had their way here as elsewhere. He notes that when Josiah reached the age of majority at 20, it would have been 'unthinkable' in the theological world of the Chronicler that he would have done nothing about the 'pagan' shrines for another six years. Thus, it was theologically desirable that Josiah begin his reform in his 12th year rather than wait until his 18th. Na'aman has also connected the dating of the reform (which he puts in 622 BCE) with the height of the crisis in Assyria during the revolt of Babylon in 626–623 BCE. It may be that the Assyrian ruler Sin-shar-ishkun's problems were sufficient to give Josiah confidence to initiate his reforms without being in danger of attracting Assyrian disapproval, while the Egyptians who replaced them may not have been particularly concerned.

Many have followed the narrative of 2 Chr. 35.20-27 which has Josiah die in a pitched battle. This seems unlikely, however, since Judah as an Egyptian vassal state is not likely to have been in a military position to challenge the Egyptian army. On the other hand, a vassal king would have been expected to appear before the new ruler (Necho II [610–595 BCE] in this case) to pay homage and swear allegiance. Doubts have been expressed about the fate of Josiah for some considerable period of time (Na'aman 1991, 51-55, with earlier literature). 2 Kings is clearly reticent to tell what happened, but Na'aman's argument that Necho had Josiah executed for suspected disloyalty of some sort makes the most sense, not only from the general historical situation but also from a close reading of the text in 2 Kings.

Reign of Jehoahaz (2 Kings 23.30-34)

Nothing is known of him, though he has only the brief reign of three months. What does fit is that he would have been removed from the throne by the Egyptians who were probably in control of the region at this time (as discussed in the previous section).

Reign of Jehoiakim (2 Kings 23.34–24.6)

Jehoiakim is known only from the biblical text, yet his reign illustrates the external politics of the ancient Near East at this time and fits in well with them. Judah was clearly an Egyptian vassal, since it was the Egyptians who put Jehoiakim on the throne. But in Jehoiakim's fourth year Nebuchadnezzar gained control of the region after the battle of Carchemish, and Judah became the vassal of the Babylonians. He then rebelled after three years. Why? The answer is that in 601 BCE Nebuchadnezzar fought a costly battle with Necho II which inflicted considerable damage on both armies; indeed, it took the Babylonians several years to recover, as indicated by Babylonican Chronicle 5 (quoted in Grabbe 2007b, 188-89). It was after this battle that Jehoiakim rebelled. It was not until two years later that Nebuchadnezzar retaliated by fostering raids against Judah, and it was not until late in 598 that he sent an army against Jerusalem.

2 Chronicles 36.6 states that Nebuchadnezzar besieged Jerusalem and took Jehoiakim captive to Babylon, while Jer. 22.18-19 predicts that he would have the 'burial of an ass' (i.e. his carcass would be dragged outside Jerusalem and left exposed and unburied). Neither appears to be what happened: from 2 Kings 24 it looks as if Jehoiakim died a natural death only a couple of months or so before Nebuchadnezzar set siege to Jerusalem, and it was his son who paid the price for his rebellion. As for Dan. 1.1-2, it is completely confused, most likely based on a misreading of the narrative in 2 Kings and 2 Chronicles (Grabbe 1987, 138-40).

Reign of Jehoiachin (2 Kings 24.6-16; 25.27-30)

Although he reigned only very briefly, Jehoiachin is well attested. In the biblical writings his name is mentioned not only in 2 Kings and 2 Chronicles but also in Jeremiah (22.24, 28; 27.20; 28.4; 29.2; 37.1; 52.31), Ezekiel (1.2), and Esther (2.6). Jehoiachin is known (though not by name) from the Babylonian Chronicles which tell of Nebuchadnezzar's taking of Jerusalem and his carrying of the Judaean king into captivity. Jehoiachin's name has also been preserved in the Jehoiachin tablets from Babylon (quoted in Grabbe 2007b, 189-90). Thus, this young ephemeral ruler is better known from extra-biblical sources than the famous Josiah.

Reign of Zedekiah (2 Kings 24.17–25.21)

The last king of Judah is known from the Babylonian Chronicles as the king placed on the throne by Nebuchadnezzar after his conquest of Jerusalem in early 597 BCE. Zedekiah's name is known only from the biblical text, however. We have no Mesopotamian historical sources after 594 when the Babylonian Chronicles come to an end. Yet the inscription of Psammetichus II (595–589 BCE) describing a tour of Palestine fits a situation in which the king of Judah was constantly looking for ways to free himself from the overlordship of Nebuchadnezzar (quoted in Grabbe 2007b, 190-91). The rebellion and final siege and capture of Jerusalem are, unfortunately, not known from any Mesopotamian source. The Egyptians were supposed to have assisted Zedekiah temporarily by sending an army, which caused the Babylonians to lift their siege, but the Egyptians withdrew, and the Babylonian siege was resumed (Jer. 37.4-11). We know nothing of this from either Babylonian or Egyptian sources.

The pharaoh at the time was Apries (589–570 BCE, called Hofrah in the biblical text [Jer. 44.30]), yet our knowledge of Pharaoh Apries from native Egyptian sources is deficient. However, we have some information from Greek sources that has generally been accepted by Egyptologists (Herodotus 2.161-69; Diodorus Siculus 1.68.1-6). According to these sources, Apries brought Phoenicia into submission. Jeremiah 27.3 indicates that Tyre and Sidon supported Zedekiah's rebellion. Apries' actions seem to fit into this context. In view of the detailed information confirmed for 2 Kings in the period before this, the reasonableness (for the most part) of the picture in 2 Kings, and the general background situation in the ancient Near East, it does not take much of a leap of faith to accept the general picture and the approximate date for the destruction of Jerusalem.

Summary of Last Days of Judah

The account of the seventh century in 2 Kings is part of the DH. The most part of the text of 2 Chronicles and some parts of Jeremiah parallel the narrative of 2 Kings. The relationship of Jeremiah to 2 Kings is not immediately apparent, but it seems plain that 2 Chronicles is mainly derived from 2 Kings; however, here and there are significant deviations. The main ones are the following:

- Manasseh's alleged captivity in Babylon and subsequent repentance is given in 2 Chr. 33.10-17 but completely absent from 2 Kings.
- 2 Chronicles (33.14), but not 2 Kings, states that Manasseh built the outer wall around part of Jerusalem.
- According to 2 Chr. 34.3-7 Josiah began the purge of 'foreign' cults in his 12th year.
- Whereas 2 Kgs 22.21-23 mentions briefly Josiah's Passover, 2 Chr. 35.1-19 goes into great detail about how it was celebrated.
- According to 2 Chr. 35.20-27 Josiah was killed in a battle with Pharaoh Necho, but 2 Kgs 23.28-30 is unspecific and does not at all imply a battle.
- According to 2 Chr. 36.6-7 Jehoiakim was taken captive to Babylon, along with the temple vessels. On the other hand, according to Jeremiah he was to have 'the burial of an ass', cast outside

Jerusalem unburied (Jer. 22.18-19). 2 Kings 24.6 implies, however, that Jehoiakim died peacefully in his bed in Jerusalem and was buried with his ancestors.

- In spite of Josiah's far-reaching reform programme described in 2 Kings and 2 Chronicles, Jeremiah seems strangely silent about it.
- Daniel 1.1-2 seems to know of Nebuchadnezzar's conquest of Jerusalem only through the biblical text. His putting the (first) siege of Jerusalem in Jehoiakim's third year is apparently based on a partial misunderstanding of 2 Chronicles. Both 2 Kings and 2 Chronicles, as well as the Babylonian Chronicles, are silent on any such taking of Jerusalem.
- As a sort of appendix to the story, the last few verses of 2 Kings (25.22-26) describe the brief governorship of Gedaliah who was assassinated by Ishmael. This Ishmael then took some Jews to Egypt. This story is given in greater detail in Jeremiah 40–44 (which is told from Jeremiah's perspective), with Jeremiah one of those taken to Egypt. None of this is found in 2 Chronicles. Some seals with the name 'Gedaliah' have been found, but there are problems with associating them with this Gedaliah; however, another seal with the inscription, 'Ishmael son of the king' has a better chance of being an authentic reference to the figure of 2 Kgs 25.25-26 and Jeremiah 40–44 (Becking 1997, 75-80), though there are some doubts about its authenticity.
- The final few verses in the book (2 Kgs 25.27-30; no parallel in 2 Chronicles) recounts Jehoiachin's release from prison. Although he evidently never returned to Judah, this seems to be pointing forward to a hope for the future and a return of captives from Babylonia.

Conclusions to Chapters 3–5

Any modern historians worth their salt would immediately recognize that not all the material in the biblical text is of the same quality. First, leaving aside for the moment the long tradition of source and redaction criticism among biblical scholars, a careful reading of this lengthy stretch of text will still detect that along with narratives giving the impression of describing unfolding events are other sorts of material that look distinctly legendary. This especially applies to stories in which the chief protagonist is a prophet. Thus, whereas the reign of Omri is described succinctly and with the prima facie appearance of factuality, the reign of Ahab is dominated by stories about the prophets Elijah and Elisha. A second point that would be obvious to a modern historian is that here and there are theological summaries and that the overall perspective is one of theological judgment (e.g., the success and failure of kings is according to whether they have been 'righteous' or 'wicked' according to the religious code of the writer). Moral judgment on rulers is not in itself unusual in ancient writings, including the Greek historians. Nevertheless, it would be noticeable to a modern historian and would need to be taken account of (see further Grabbe 2001).

When we ask about 1 and 2 Kings and history, we ask a complicated question. David had effected a union of the two separate entities of Israel and Judah. Although he ruled territory a lot less extensive than alleged by 1 and 2 Samuel, he passed this polity on to Solomon. Suddenly, despite no further conquests of his own, Solomon is claimed to rule a great empire that practically controlled the whole eastern Mediterranean. This is incredible: it neither fits the resources of David's legacy nor the indications in the extra-biblical literature. Yet the text suggests that Solomon managed to hang onto the heritage from David and to keep it together throughout his reign (or at least most of it), but after his death (or possibly in his latter days) this fell apart into the two naturally separate entities of Israel and Judah.

By the ninth century we seem to have a reached a period for which there is more agreement about the general outline of history in Palestine. There appears to be general agreement that Omri and Ahab ruled over some sort of state, even if the exact nature of that state is still debated (H.M. Niemann 2007, for example, refers to Omri as the war leader of a military administration). Judah was also a separate entity, but whether it is called a state is more controversial: it might have been a vassal of Israel, which in turn was a vassal of Damascus part of the time, though not under Omri (Knauf 2007). Jerusalem could well have been much what it was in the Amarna period, perhaps more of a city-state than anything else. Most seem to agree, though, that sometime in the eighth century Judah had become a territorial state.

In the ninth century the brief hiatus of freedom from the major powers, that Palestine had enjoyed since Egypt withdrew, came to an end. Shoshenq seems to have conducted some sort of excursion(s) into Palestine, though the extent and the effects are currently moot, but in any case he did not stay. But then in the early ninth century Assyria began to make excursions to the west, and in the middle of the century are the repeated clashes between Shalmaneser III and a coalition of twelve kings from the Syro-Palestinian region, led by Damascus but with Ahab an important ally. According to the Assyrian inscriptions the coalition remained intact at least up to Shalmaneser's 14th year (845 BCE).

This is not the picture of the biblical text, which has Israel dominated by the Aramaeans and ignores the Assyrians altogether. Between Shalmaneser's 14th and his 18th year (841 BCE) things must have fallen apart, for in 841 the coalition was defeated, and with Hadadezer now dead Damascus, under a new king Hazael, alone faced the Assyrian army. In the same year the new king of Israel Jehu submitted to Assyria, putting it on the opposite side from the Aramaeans. The Assyrians continued to cause problems for Hazael for another three years, until Shalmaneser's 21st year, but then Assyria ceased to concern itself with the western part of its empire for the next thirty years. This left Damascus a free hand to dominate the region, including Israel, first under the leadership of Hazael and then under his son Bar-Hadad. This is exactly the picture of the biblical text (2 Kgs 10.34-36; 12.18-19; 13.3, 22-25).

After the events around 800 BCE, there is not a lot of further extra-biblical information for the next half century until the reign of Tiglath-pileser III. The biblical text assigns a good deal of important activity to Jeroboam II, but this individual is not mentioned by any extra-biblical sources. About 780–775 BCE, Shamshi-ilu, the Assyrian commander for the region, collected tribute from Ḥadiiāni. This would suggest that Damascus was not able to do just anything it wished. The next king of Israel mentioned is Menahem, in Tiglath-pileser's *Annals* and in the Iran Stele III (ca. 738). For the first time in the Assyrian annals, we also find a mention of the kingdom of Judah, in Tiglath-pileser's Summary Inscription 7. According to Summary Inscription 4 the Assyrian king also annexed Gilead, Galilee, and other areas of northern Israel (cf. 2 Kgs 15.29).

The Syro-Ephramite war in 734–732 BCE is not mentioned as such in the Assyrian records, but it is indirectly attested. The exact cause of Damascus and Israel ganging up on Judah still escapes us, but a number of biblical passages presuppose it. It also brought Judah into Assyria's sphere, though this was likely to have happened shortly, anyway. It presaged the final fall of the Northern Kingdom. Here again the original sources give more than one picture. Was Samaria captured by Shalmaneser V or Sargon II? The proposal that it was taken twice—in 722 and again in 720 BCE—has merit, but there are other explanations, such as Sargon claiming to capture the city when all he did was deport its inhabitants. But the basic picture of the biblical text seems to be in harmony with the Assyrian sources, even if the details are not always reliable.

With the reign of Hezekiah we have a considerable amount of extra-biblical data, especially from Assyrian sources with regard to the invasion of Sennacherib in 701 BCE. The biblical text of 2 Kgs 18.13-16 agrees closely with the Assyrian texts, though the rest of the biblical account does not. In order to salvage the biblical account, some have theorized that there were two invasions of Sennacherib, even though no evidence for such occurs in the Assyrian evidence. This is now generally rejected and considered disproved. A reference to Manasseh as paying tribute is also found in the Assyrian texts. The account in 2 Chr. 33.10-13 (but not in 2 Kings) that Manasseh was taken to Babylon by Sennacherib but released is not impossible, but then why was it not mentioned by the compilers of Kings? It seems unlikely that he would deliberately have omitted it.

When it comes to Josiah, we have the surprising fact that no mention of him is found outside the biblical text; however, the Assyrian empire was rapidly withdrawing from the west, and the Egyptian texts were not generally as helpful with historical data. Yet there are good reasons at this point to accept that the biblical text has roots in history. An analysis of the text suggests that there is a core to Josiah's religious reforms, though they were much less extensive than the present text suggests. As for Josiah's death, a careful reading of the text in Kings suggests that Josiah was executed by Pharaoh Necho. This fits the situation much better than the account in 2 Chr. 35.20-27 that has Josiah meeting Necho in battle.

The coincidence of history and the biblical text is made even clearer in the Judahite rulers after Josiah, where for several years we have detailed historical information. Indeed, there are times that we can write the history of Judah almost year by year in the decade between 605 and 594 BCE (at which point the Babylonian Chronicles cease). Nebuchadnezzar's first taking of Jerusalem is found in both the Babylonian Chronicles and the biblical text, but the events between 601 BCE and 597 BCE fit very well what we know about the history at the time. There are no extra-biblical references to the final fall of Jerusalem 587/586 BCE, but the extent of knowledge that the biblical writer seems to have at this point gives us some confidence that things happened much as recounted, at least in broad terms.

Overall, the historical data in the biblical account seem to increase gradually as one goes through the DH. In the early period, there is little that we can have confidence in with regard to Joshua and Judges. Probably more can be found in 1 and 2 Samuel, though much here cannot be relied on (see further Grabbe 2016). The data seem to increase as we go through 1 and 2 Kings, even though there is much material of dubious historical value, until toward the end of the Kingdom of Judah when quite a bit seems to be preserved. This is only a general trend, however, and each individual passage has to be studied on its own merits, and any historical conclusions have to be grounded in solid data and arguments.

Chapter 6

CONCLUSIONS:
THE BOOKS OF KINGS
IN HERMENEUTICAL PERSPECTIVE

At the end of Chapter 5 we concluded that, while the text of 1 and 2 Kings had reliable data at some points, it also contained much legendary or even completely non-historical material, especially in the prophetic legends and the theological expansions. What can we conclude about historicity at this point?

The Books of Kings as History

At first blush, books such as 1 and 2 Kings have much in common with some of the Greek historians. One important resemblance is the system of chronological indications found at various points in the text. As noted in Chapter 1 Thucydides' devising of the precise chronological placement of various events was an important development in history writing. The biblical narratives do not have such precise dating for the most part, but they are not that different from writers such as Herodotus who write about past history rather than contemporary events (Thucydides wrote about his own times).

Writers such as Herodotus also made use of a good deal of traditional lore from Egypt, Mesopotamia, Persia, and Greece itself. This material was of uneven quality from a modern perspective. Sometimes it was clearly good quality from a historical point of view; at other times we would want to put it in the category of legend (see Chapter 1, pp. 9-14). We could probably make the same statement about material in the Deuteronomistic History. Some of it contains examples of reliable traditions, but other parts of it are clearly legendary and would not be accepted as having much to do with history by most critical scholars.

This has led some to argue that the DtrH can be a historian as much as the Greek historians, as for example Baruch Halpern. One of his arguments is that the DtrH has used sources. He admits that there is invention of data or non-historical material but insists on the essential source basis of the work: 'DtrH bases itself, if partly on historical imagination, heavily on antiquarian research' (Halpern 1988, 216). There seems no question that for 1 and 2 Kings the compiler used some sort of source which sometimes contained reliable information on the kings of Israel and Judah. The suggestion that the compiler has gone around copying the data from monuments, however, is not very credible (Halpern 1988, 208-9, 215; Van Seters 1983, 298, 301, 357), if for no other reason than that the number of monumental inscriptions is not likely to have been high. Also, it was not the custom of ancient historians to collect such data (Momigliano 1966; Veyne 1988, 8).

More credible is the suggestion that a court or temple chronicle was used. Such a chronicle preserved in Jerusalem, for example, would probably give the main accomplishments of a particular ruler, significant invasions or domination by a foreign king, and some events relating to the neighbouring kingdom of Israel. That the writer had other sources is also credible, but whether they were as numerous or of as good quality as Halpern assumes is questionable (1988, 207-16). He asserts, 'Most scholars concede that H(Dtr) had a rich fund of materials', but 'rich fund' is not the same as accurate or reliable. Some of this rich fund was prophetic legends that scarcely count as dependable historical sources.

Whether the compiler used sources is not the main issue, however. Unless the writer completely invented everything, he must have used sources: legends, tales, hearsay, oral tradition, court stories. Two questions remain: First, did he make use of primary sources? By 'primary sources' I mean those that are close to the actual events in time and connection. The historian should, where possible, work from primary sources, but that is often not possible for antiquity. However, the Bible is not normally a primary source. Most of the time, it is clear that the text was written long after the events being discussed (though the use of a court chronicle in some cases brings us much closer to a primary source). The second question is how he worked: What was his aim, and did he exercise critical judgment? These are important questions, but Halpern's concern seems simply to give him 'antiquarian interests'. This may be true, but what was his overall aim? Was it to write an accurate reconstruction of past history or was it to give a theological interpretation to which historical data and aims took a back seat?

I see no evidence that the DtrH exercised critical historical judgment as we normally understand it. The enquiry into all sources of information, the critical evaluation of sources, the testing for bias and ideological colouring, the scepticism toward explanations contrary to normal experience are all elements within modern historical study and reconstruction. The Greeks questioned their myths and traditions in a way for which we have no evidence among Jewish historians. The answer to the question of the DtrH's aim seems to be obvious, as Halpern himself evidently accepts when he refers to 'DtrH: a cultic interpretation of history' (1988, 220). The author has indeed exercised judgment, but it was theological judgment. The question of theological motivation has thus become a very important one at this point (cf. the perceptive comments of Hans M. Barstad 1998). We need now to take a look at the theology question.

The Books of Kings and Theology

We can begin with the classic *Old Testament Theology* by Gerhard von Rad (1962–65). He emphasized Yhwh's 'continuing divine activity in history. This implies that in principle Israel's faith is grounded in a theology of history' (1962–65, 1:106). By the time von Rad's work appeared, the Biblical Theology Movement was at its peak (for an account of its rise, characteristics, and decline, see Childs 1970). The Biblical Theology Movement became a very popular movement in the 1950s and 1960s. This emphasis on history fitted well into its perspective. Both the Biblical Theology Movement promoter G. Ernest Wright and von Rad regarded Yhwh's 'divine acts in history' as the chief mode of revelation and the core of Old Testament theology.

However, the language used by proponents of the Biblical Theology Movement was capable of being misunderstood. They often spoke as if they accepted a literal interpretation of the biblical account, including the supernatural and miraculous elements of the stories. Von Rad makes it clear that by 'history' he means those events as interpreted by the faith of Israel 'and not of the results of modern critical historical scholarship... Critical historical scholarship regards it as impossible that...Israel crossed the Red Sea and achieved the Conquest *en bloc*' (1962–65, 1:106-7). Advocates of the Biblical Theology Movement, such as G. Ernest Wright, took a similar view, though this was not always as clear as it was with von Rad.

In other words, what was often meant by 'history' was not history as understood by modern critical historians but a type of *Heilsgeschichte* or 'history of salvation'. 'History' was simply the narrative of events as understood by ancient Israel, who remembered the past as the result of God's actions and decisions. The 'mighty acts of God in history' were Israel's cultural memory about what God had done and which was recounted to subsequent generations. But this is not history as critical historians know it; this is theology. Steven Holladay agrees that the books of Kings form a 'theological history; it does not attempt to offer an objective or dispassionate reportage of the "facts"' (1992, 4:79).

James Barr wrote extensively on the subject of the Hebrew Bible, theology, and history. His critique of the Biblical Theology Movement's view of history has been widely accepted (see especially Barr 1965, 65-102; 1980, 1-17). A very important point that he makes is that the narratives in 1 and 2 Kings are not history but 'history-like' (1980, 5). Their most important characteristic is 'story' (1980, 5-10; 1999, 345-61). This argument that the best way to characterize much of 1 and 2 Kings is 'story' is very promising for understanding the books and developing methods for understanding their contents.

It is true that some still worry about abandoning 'history' as a *sine qua non* of the biblical text. Granted, when students begin to study the books of Kings, their reading is often dominated by an academic perspective which—traditionally—has looked at the books primarily as historiography. We have devoted plenty of time to historiography, but it is salutary to remind ourselves that the books of Kings were read for many centuries as theology—and as story. Of course, readers would have assumed that the stories were a real account of the past, but their interest was in the lessons that could be learned, the examples for behaviour and conduct, the teachings about religion and morality, and the evaluations of different figures assumed to be actual historical personages who said and did what the biblical text stated.

Over many centuries the Bible was the only book that many Jews and Christians knew. Indeed, they may not have known it as a book, either because they did not possess a copy or could not read, but the contents of the Bible were widespread through the various communities because of teachings through synagogue or church. The biblical stories were taught to children and became a part of communal knowledge. Now, literary and theological readings of 1 and 2 Kings have also become an important aspect of biblical scholarship. This does not stop us from asking historical questions, but if our answer is negative, this does not remove the value of the text. Viewing the text as 'story' has great potential for seeing its value in areas other than history. An a-historical or non-historical interpretation of the text can have quite positive implications. We are ready to look at examples of where the text has other valuable messages.

Good Kings and Bad Kings

In the books of Kings there are many stories. In most cases, there are theological judgments about whether the king at a particular time was righteous or wicked, or whether his reign was good or bad. There are often other theological statements about the reign of the king in question. Wicked kings are usually said to have tolerated the presence of high places for worship among the people (e.g., 1 Kgs 3.2; 12.31-32; 2 Kgs 16.4). Surprisingly, though, some kings are designated as righteous, even though it is admitted that they did not remove the high places (1 Kgs 15.14; 22.44; 2 Kgs 12.4; 14.4; 15.4, 35); indeed, it is only in the time of Hezekiah that the high places are first said to have been removed by a king (2 Kgs 18.4). The reason seems to lie in the development of Israelite religion, which we can discuss now.

As was already noted several times in Chapters 3–5, what we find in a number of the theological statements are assumptions about Israelite religion that appear to be anachronistic. That is, religion in Israel, and then Judah, had developed in a certain way through the centuries. It eventually became monotheistic, aniconic, lacking a female consort, with a centralized cult place (for a discussion and references, see Grabbe 2007b, 150-63). The final developments seem to have been in the late monarchy, the Neo-Babylonian, and the Persian periods (without at this point trying to be specific about the exact timing of specific developments). Although the text ascribes cult centralization to Hezekiah, this is widely doubted now (Grabbe 2007b, 195-96; also above pp. 68-69); in my view, Hezekiah's 'reforms' were primarily political, linked to his desire to break away from Assyrian rule. It was under Josiah that the cult was centralized in Jerusalem and the high places abolished in Judah (Hezekiah's actions were interpreted by later editors as religious, drawing on the model of Josiah).

But in the mind of the Deuteronomistic editor, the presence of high places at an earlier time was nothing but a sign of religious apostasy. So were other practices that were apparently remembered from the past, even though at the time they were a normal part of the religious scene. If one takes a broader view (including the evidence of archaeology), Israelite worship looks very much at home among the other Semitic religions, especially those of the Northwest Semitic region. This is not to deny that Israelite worship developed unique characteristics and came to establish strong boundaries against other religions, but this took a long time to develop.

The deity most frequently and strongly associated with ancient Israel is Yhwh. He appears to have been a national or ethnic god, much as Chemosh was the god of the Moabites, Qaus the god of the Edomites, and so on (cf. 1 Kgs 11.33). This does not mean that Yhwh was the only god worshiped in the kingdoms of Israel and Judah, but he seems to have been the main object of devotion. His is the name most widely attested.

The references to the God of Israel in the biblical text do not just contain the name Yhwh. Many other names and titles occur, though often translated in Bible translations as epithets or descriptions rather than rendered as names. For example, the name *El* is used of the Israelite God but can also mean just 'god' in a generic sense. This is in line with much Northwest Semitic usage in which *el* (or the earlier form *ilu*) could stand both for the head of the pantheon (the god El) and for the word 'god, divinity' in general. The name El Shaddai (or just Shaddai alone) is also used in a number of passages in Genesis (17.1; 28.3; 35.11; 48.3; 49.25).

Other biblical texts also suggest a time when Yhwh was not only a deity alongside other deities but perhaps even a subordinate of El. Scholars had long wondered whether the reading of the Hebrew text of Deut. 32.8 was not due to a later editing because of the Septuagint text which seemed to presuppose a different Hebrew original. The suggestion of another more original Hebrew reading seems now to have been confirmed by a Hebrew manuscript from Qumran (4QDeut^j = 4Q37), which reads '[according to the number of] the sons of God' (*bny 'lhym*). The passage goes on to say that Jacob is Yhwh's portion (Deut. 32.9). All of these data suggest that the passage originally read something along the lines of the following:

> When Elyon gave the inheritence of the nations,
> When he divided the sons of Adam (or man),
> He established the boundaries of the peoples
> According to the number of the sons of El.
> For Yhwh's lot is his people
> And Jacob his inherited portion.

This suggests that Yhwh (as one of these sons of El) inherited Israel as his particular portion. Such a situation in which Yhwh is merely one among the sons of El in the divine assembly is found in Ps. 89.7-8 which reads literally:

> For who in heaven compares to Yhwh?
> Who is like Yhwh among the sons of the Elim (gods)?
> El creates awe in the council of the Holy Ones.
> He is great and strikes fear in all about him.

Here Yhwh is a son of El, among other sons, even if he is said to be incomparable to his fellow sons of El. Similarly, Ps. 82.1 speaks of God (Elohim) judging among the gods in the divine assembly.

A number of other passages also give a mythical picture of Yhwh not found in most biblical texts (Day 1985). These passages suggest that God created by defeating various monsters of chaos who appear as supernatural beings. For example, in Isa. 27.1 Yhwh takes his sword and defeats 'Leviathan (*lwytn*) the piercing (*brḥ*) serpent, even Leviathan the slippery (*'qltwn*) serpent, and he will slay the Tannin (*tnyn*) in the sea'. This can be compared with Ugaritic texts which allege that Baal defeated such monsters (e.g., *KTU* 2; 1.3.3.37-42; 1.5.1.1-3).

These various passages are isolated survivals of older beliefs which had been obliterated or reinterpreted by the dominant monotheistic view of Yhwh that controlled the final shaping of the biblical text. A few verses escaped editing, however, confirming what we now know from inscriptions: Yhwh was originally conceived as one god among many, perhaps even subordinate to and a son of El. He created by fighting and defeating various monsters of chaos, such as Leviathan, Tannin, and Rahab, much as Baal did in the Ugaritic texts. When monotheism became the dominant view in Israel and Judah, these older views were simply expunged or, in some cases, they were reinterpreted so as not to be an embarrassment to monotheistic views.

Biblical names also suggest a plethora of deities. Many biblical names are theophorous, i.e., they have a divine name within them. For example, the name Elijah contains both the divine name El and the divine name Yah (a shortened form of Yhwh). The names with El are too numerous to mention (Israel, Elijah, Elisha, Samuel, and so on); more significant are Shaddai (e.g., Num. 1.5-6: Shedeur, Zurishaddai; Num. 1.12: Ammishaddai). But perhaps most interesting are the names with Baal. Considering the biblical polemic against Baal, one might have expected not to see such names, but they are found in surprising contexts. One of Saul's sons has a name compounded with Baal: Eshbaal ('man of Baal') and Jonathan's son was Meribbaal. These names are often overlooked because the Samuel texts actually substitute surrogate names compounded with the word 'shame' (Ishbosheth [2 Sam. 2.8]; Mephibosheth [2 Sam. 21.7]), but they are correctly preserved in 1 Chronicles (8.33-34; 9.39-40). Some documents written on pot sherds found during the excavation of Samaria (referred to as the 'Samaria ostraca') have names of local people, some of which are theophorous. They give a similarly mixed picture, since it appears that Baal and Yhwh were worshipped happily side by side: about half the theophorous names contain a form of Yhwh and half contain a form of Baal.

At various points in the text, it is stated that a king did or did not remove the *qᵉdēšîm* from the land. This term has often been translated as 'male cult prostitute', but this is now generally rejected: there is little or no evidence of cult prostitution (whether male or female) in Canaanite religion, as was once assumed. The *qᵉdēšîm* were probably cult personnel of some sort. We know that among the cult personnel at Ugarit were individuals called *qdšm*, yet there is no evidence for ritual prostitution—male or female—at Ugarit. In contrast to the older consensus that took cultic prostitution for granted, the existence of such an institution has been widely questioned in recent years: there is little support for the oft-repeated assertion that cultic prostitution formed a part of the non-Yahwistic cults. (For a discussion and bibliography, see Grabbe 2015.)

Perhaps most revealing are recent finds that suggest that Yhwh once had a consort. Inscriptions found in 1975–76 at Kuntillet Ajrud in the Negev (dated about the eighth century BCE) is conventionally read, 'I blessed you by Yhwh of Samaria and by his Asherah'. Similarly, in Khirbet el-Qom near Hebron, another inscription was found and dated to the seventh century and has been read in a similar manner. These finds have created a great deal of debate because this is the first time that any direct evidence of goddess worship had turned up (even the Samaria ostraca had no goddess names). After considerable disagreement, the consensus is moving definitely in the direction of seeing a consort alongside Yhwh, a female divinity called Asherah (even if not everyone agrees). If so, this would be quite parallel to Ugarit in which El the head of the pantheon has Athirat (cognate with Hebrew Asherah) as his consort. Jeremiah (44.17-19, 25) mentions worship of the 'Queen of Heaven' who is likely to have been Asherah or Anat or perhaps even an amalgam of the two goddesses. Yet even though the text presents these as acts of apostasy, there is no hint that such worship was criticized or opposed at the time. If there was criticism, it was likely to have been a minority movement, perhaps a 'Yhwh-alone movement' (as argued by Morton Smith 1971).

How early monotheism developed is very much a point of dispute, though the general view today is that it was fairly late. The final form of the text in most biblical books bears the stamp of those who were apparently monotheistic. In the biblical text Yhwh is clearly equated with El and with other divine names. Since Asherah is most often a consort of El in Northwest Semitic texts, a number of recent scholars have suggested that this equation is not fortuitous but represents the actual origin of Yhwh, i.e., that the latter developed in the context of El worship. In any case, it would not be surprising for El and Yhwh to be assimilated over time even if they were once separate deities. The various other male deities are equated with Yhwh (except for Baal who is depicted as in a life-or-death struggle with Yhwh). This is a part of the process of moving toward monotheism. Many would argue that we find monotheism already in Second Isaiah with his denial of the existence of other gods (e.g., Albertz 1994, 417-18; Smith 2001, 179-94; 2002, 191-99): Yhwh alone is without beginning or end, uniquely divine and God alone, the creator of the cosmos, and there is nothing like him (Isa. 46.9; 48.12-13).

Thus, many scholars see the development of monotheism—in some circles, anyway—during the seventh–sixth centuries BCE. For example, it has been pointed out that astral imagery of the late eighth and seventh centuries had disappeared from seals and seal impressions of the Jerusalem elite by the early sixth and also the blessing and salvation functions of Yhwh's 'Asherah', known from several inscriptions, had been absorbed by Yhwh by the time of the Lachish and Arad ostraca (Uehlinger 1995, 2005). This has been interpreted as indirect evidence of Josiah's reform and a move in the direction of monotheism.

Other Interpretations of the 'Story'

Our investigation of the development of Israelite religion is another reason why the text can be interpreted by methods other than historical ones. As we have argued, the concept of 'story' fits much of the material in Kings. But the story (narrative) is only the raw material for theology. The stories have to be interpreted. Sometimes the text itself gives us an interpretation, but this is limited to the interests of the Deuteronomistic editors. This has not restricted interpreters of later periods from finding meaning in these stories to fit their own age and interests. This is the task of *hermeneutics*—to find meaning in the ancient text for contemporary concerns of modern readers. The central concerns of the text (which were the concerns of the ancient authors and editors) may not be our concerns. We may in fact find them not just irrelevant but even repugnant. Thus, the ancient text sometimes focused on issues that do not interest us or at least are not in the forefront of our interests.

For example, the Deuteronomistic writers and editors were especially concerned about cultic matters (e.g., the 'high places'), and the right or wrong observance of certain rites occupies a large part of the text and often forms the criterion for judging righteousness or wickedness. Yet most of us are not so concerned about such cultic issues. We no longer make blood sacrifice the centre of our worship, making the arguments for a central temple redundant today. Most of us expect to worship in a local church or synagogue or religious congregation of some sort; the text's preoccupation with the Jerusalem temple has little concern for us.

Rather than cultic matters, we are more often concerned with what we consider ethical matters. Ethical concerns are there in the ancient text, of course, though sometimes in the background or best expressed through examples. It is right and proper from a hermeneutical point of view to give preference to issues that we are concerned with.

Indeed, in some cases—few, we hope—we might actually reject the concern or view of the text. For example, most of us consider religious tolerance very important, yet the text is mostly very intolerant of any religious belief or practice that differs from the strict Deuteronomistic list. Things they tolerated, such as slavery, negative views about women, persecution of certain beliefs, and so on we would consider unacceptable. Yet this does not prevent us from learning from the text and having our thoughts stimulated by it. From a hermeneutical point of view, the purpose of the text is not to indoctrinate us or tell us what to believe but to make us think. Only some examples can be given here, but they will illustrate some of the approaches of contemporary scholars and theologians.

An approach that has occupied the attention of many modern interpreters is *reader response*. Like other hermeneutical methods, it seeks to make the text relevant for modern readers. What it does is direct the reader to react to the biblical story in light of his or her interests and background. That is, the interpretative engagement and the conclusions will vary from interpreter to interpreter, depending on such matters as education, religious affiliation, class, gender, sexual orientation—all the elements of one's background and character. Although the formal recognition of this mode of interpretation may be recent, it has been going on for centuries, even if unconsciously.

With regard to the books of Kings, the church and synagogue have used the stories contained in the books as examples in teaching and preaching. They could be treated as models or paradigms of behaviour to be imitated or avoided. In many cases, explicit theological statements or interpretations accompany the story but, as noted above, we are not obligated to interpret the story as the original editors did. Also, sometimes even the implications of the story in question are left to the reader.

An interesting book to begin with is Joseph Blenkinsopp's *David Remembered* (2013). His concern is not the historical David in 1 and 2 Samuel and the first chapter of 1 Kings but the David tradition as it was remembered, interpreted, and applied in new situations by biblical interpreters. He traces how the David tradition was commemorated and reused from the last days of the kingdom of Judah, through Zerubbabel and Nehemiah, through the prophetic expectation of a future king like David, to the concept of a protective Davidic messiah in the Roman period and, finally, Jesus as a Davidic descendant. For example, Josiah seems to have been modelled as a new David. In the restoration of the early Persian period Zerubbabel took on a number of the characteristics of a Davidic ruler. Of course, the concept of a messiah was based on the image of David (though we know that with time priestly elements entered the tradition). Finally, Jesus in the New Testament is the 'son of David', which is not just a paper title but an indication of having many of the attributes of David and the Davidic rulers.

Blenkinsopp's study is an example of a fairly recent scholarly preoc-cupation, *reception history* (sometimes referred to by the German term *Wirkungsgeschichte*). This is the investigation of how a text has been interpreted (or even mis-interpreted) in the past, whether by scholars or in church or synagogue. Studies of reception history can be combined with reader response, since the way the text has been previously inter-preted has often brought it closer to the modern reader. Also, the religious background of the reader might make the person more receptive to an interpretation compatible with their own religious tradition.

Another form of reader response that has been around for some time, especially since the 1970s, is *feminist criticism*. The problem with Kings is that there are only a few female characters in the two books, though the *Women's Bible Commentary* (edited by Carol A. Newsom and Sharon H. Ringe, 1998) has comments on these books, as on all books of the Bible. One of the central characters is, of course, Jezebel. She is presented very negatively in the text and has been interpreted negatively through the ages. But some recent studies have recognized the bias of this picture, not because of a feminist bias but because of realizing that the text and inter-pretations were themselves prejudiced and also failed to understand the background to the context in which Jezebel lived (see, e.g., Pruin 2006, 2007). At the beginning of 1 Kings, Bath-Sheba is a part of the final events of the David story and the beginning of Solomon's reign. Bath-Sheba has been the subject of a number of feminist studies (such as in Exum 1996). Patricia Dutcher-Walls looked at Athaliah and 2 Kings 11–12 using a variety of analytical methods (1996). The other main female figure in Kings is the prophetess Huldah, who was consulted by Josiah over the book found in the temple (2 Kgs 22.14); she was remembered by the rabbis many centuries later (Ilan 2010).

One recent method that can be applied to texts such as 1 and 2 Kings is *postcolonial* analysis. A recent work that includes ancient Israel is Leo Perdue and Warren Carter, *Israel and Empire: A Postcolonial History of Israel and Early Judaism* (2015). The concerns are what we would expect, though sometimes the vocabulary and terminology might be new. Of special interest are the various modes of subjugation used by the colonizing power, not just force and power but also propaganda, ceremonies, education, and even religion. Also considered are the ways in which the 'subalterns' (those colonized or subjugated) resist, including not only through revolution but also resistance writing. A number of inner-discipline debates have taken place, but the main one that concerns us is the fact that the colonial model followed is primarily that of the nineteenth and early twentieth century. It is evident that in broad outline the model can be applied to antiquity, but many details differ. It would be a mistake to extrapolate some aspects of recent colonialism to the empires of the ancient world. This will become clearer as more studies using this method are published, reviewed, and debated. We also often know too little about ancient empires to make reliable judgments (cf. Perdue and Carter 2015, 129-31).

We also have some specific studies of individual kings, some of which might serve as useful examples. Mostly, writers have focused on 'righteous' kings, such as Hezekiah and Josiah. The first is Hezekiah, about whom we have much more information than is normal for kings of Judah. Nevertheless, there is still a lot not known and there are many historical problems with the small amount of information we do have. R.A. Young, *Hezekiah in History and Tradition* (2012), provides a reworking of what may be asserted about the historical Hezekiah. He gives what might be called a maximalist reconstruction from the sources, and many readers will not be able to follow him in all his conclusions, e.g., that there was greater literacy under Hezekiah, or that he instituted a religious reform (and that the description is not just a duplication of the Josianic reform). Yet his reconstruction is based on a careful critical examination of the data and provides a solid base on which to build further study of this fascinating period in Judah's history. A welcome reassessment of Manasseh was given by Percy Van Keulen in *Manasseh through the Eyes of the Deuteronomists* (1996), who also compared the Kings account with that in Chronicles.

Marvin Sweeney wrote *King Josiah of Judah: The Lost Messiah of Israel* (2001) which argues that Josiah sought to be anointed king (messiah) of a restored united kingdom of Israel with Jerusalem and the temple at its centre. His experiment failed with his death at Megiddo; nevertheless, his dream was remembered and left its mark on a variety of books and passages. Sweeney argues that Josiah became the model for a restored Davidic monarchy, yet his failure meant that some were already

abandoning the idea of a restored monarchy even before the time of
Zerubbabel, and the final form of the DH (exilic period) calls the role of
the Davidic house into question. This book bears on the question of using
the biblical text in reconstructing Israelite history.

A final example of an Israelite king concerns Jeroboam (I) who is
presented so negatively in the biblical text, because of splitting the
kingdom of David and Solomon. Keith Bodner's electing to write on
Jeroboam's Royal Drama (2012) is a rather striking choice, even an
inspired one. It is primarily a reading of the Jeroboam story but consti-
tutes a character study in a larger discourse of power. Reminiscent of
postcolonialism Bodner's study discusses the legitimacy of rebellion.
Going beyond Israel, even the Aramaean king Hazael is seen as having
an important theological function in the books of Kings, according to
Hadi Ghantous's *The Elisha–Hazael Paradigm and the Kingdom of Israel*
(2013). Along with a study of the historical Hazael, this investigation
considers the 'Elisha–Hazael paradigm' in the Hebrew Bible, by which
is meant Yhwh's mysterious action in using Hazael as a tool to punish
Israel and Judah. In the literature of the Hebrew Bible, Hazael 'provided
a theological interpretative paradigm to grapple with the political misfor-
tunes of the kingdoms of Israel and Judah' (Ghantous 2013, 184).

Conclusions

The chapters of this book have explored a number of issues relating to the
books of 1 and 2 Kings. We ultimately depend on a Hebrew text of the
book, though whether this is best represented by the traditional Jewish
Hebrew text (MT) or perhaps more indirectly by one of the Greek versions
known today (such as the Lucianic version) is still a matter of debate.
But for most purposes, the differences between these two texts does not
seriously affect some of the broader questions we have considered (such
as the concern about whether the text can be called 'historical' or not). The
books of 1 and 2 Kings are still widely seen as part of a broader collection
of books, known as the Deuteronomistic History (DH), which includes
at least the books of Joshua, Judges, and 1 and 2 Samuel. Many still
view these as parts of a unified composition that begins with the book of
Deuteronomy, very much in accord with the thesis of Martin Noth, though
others wonder whether the DH is anything more than a loose collection of
books. Many also date the DH to the early or mid-Babylonian period in
the sixth century BCE, even if a significant number of scholars think an
early edition arose during the late seventh century, in the time of Josiah

(though it may have been expanded and edited in the early sixth century BCE). Again, the differences in dating do not seem to have major implications about the question of historicity.

Much of our study focused on these important questions of history and historiography. Can the books of Kings (or even the whole DH) be called 'history'? If so, in what sense? Only in a loose sense, as showing an interest in the past? In a critical sense, at least comparable to the historians of ancient Greece? Can the miraculous elements be confirmed, or at least the notion that the history of Israel features the 'might acts of God'? Do these books constitute history, whereas the other writings of the ancient Near East are only examples of myth or legend?

Our examination of the text from a historiographical point of view in Chapters 3–5 gave us at least part of the answer: the text of Kings contains many historical data that could be used in writing a history but much of the text is also non-historical from a modern point of view. Unlike history writing as it developed in the Greco-Roman period (though not all Hellenistic writers about history rose to a very high level compared to Thucydides or the Oxyrhynchus Historian [see p. 12 on him]), the DH shows no evidence of applying critical thought or analysis and its ultimate aim was theological, not the telling of history. We cannot consider the DH as 'history' in the same sense as modern critical history or even in the sense as written by Herodotus or Polybius.

Yet the value of 1 and 2 Kings is and has always been theological. Analysis has shown these books to be 'history-like' rather than historical. Their primary character is *story*. Once we recognize this, we can move to other methods of understanding and accessing the writings. Examples of several of these were noted (reader response and related disciplines, feminist criticism, postcolonial analysis, reception history, ethics and morality, and of course various other aspects of theology). Most readers will ultimately have a hermeneutical concern: What does the text mean to me/us in my/our situation in the present time? The various methods mentioned, plus others, can help us in the hermeneutical task. These can of course be combined with historical analysis.

If your interest is in history, there is much still to be gleaned from 1 and 2 Kings: our task of evaluating them historically is far from finished. But even if you have no interest at all in history, these books are still an important part of the Bible and have messages for all readers. They will greatly repay careful study—and they are filled with interesting stories.

BIBLIOGRAPHY

Albertz, Rainer. 1994. *A History of Israelite Religion in the Old Testament Period*, 2 vols. London: SCM.

———. 2005. 'Why a Reform Like Josiah's Must Have Happened'. Pages 27-46 in Grabbe 2005.

Ash, Paul S. 1999. *David, Solomon and Egypt: A Reassessment*. JSOTSup 297. Sheffield Academic.

Athas, George. 2003. *The Tel Dan Inscription: A Reappraisal and a New Interpretation*. JSOTSup 360. Copenhagen International Seminar 12. Sheffield Academic.

Avioz, Michael. 2005. 'The Book of Kings in Recent Research (Part I)'. *CBR* 4:11-55.

———. 2006. 'The Book of Kings in Recent Research (Part II)'. *CBR* 5:11-57.

Balcer, Jack Martin. 1987. *Herodotus and Bisitun: Problems in Ancient Persian Historiography*. Historia Einzelschriften 49. Stuttgart: Steiner.

Barr, James. 1965. *Old and New in Interpretation: A Study of the Two Testaments*. London: SCM.

———. 1980. *The Scope and Authority of the Bible*. London: SCM. Philadelphia: Westminster.

———. 1999. *The Concept of Biblical Theology: An Old Testament Perspective*. London: SCM, 1999.

Barstad, Hans M. 1998. 'The Strange Fear of the Bible: Some Reflections on the "Bibliophobia" in Recent Ancient Israelite Historiography'. Pages 120-27 in *Leading Captivity Captive: 'The Exile' as History and Ideology*. Edited by Lester L. Grabbe. JSOTSup 278 = ESHM 2. Sheffield: Sheffield Academic, 1998.

Barthélemy, Dominique. 1963. *Les devanciers d'Aquila*. VTSup 10. Leiden: Brill.

Becking, Bob. 1992. *The Fall of Samaria: An Historical and Archaeological Study*. Studies in the History of the Ancient Near East 2. Leiden: Brill.

———. 1997. 'Inscribed Seals as Evidence for Biblical Israel? Jeremiah 40.7–41.15 *Par Exemple*'. Pages 65-83 in *Can a "History of Israel" Be Written?* Edited by Lester L. Grabbe. JSOTSup 245 = ESHM 1. Sheffield: Sheffield Academic.

———. 2002. 'West Semites at Tell Šēḫ Ḥamad: Evidence for the Israelite Exile?'. Pages 153-66 in *Kein Land für sich allein: Studien zum Kulturkontakt in Kanaan, Israel/ Palästina und Ebirnâri für Manfred Weippert zum 65. Geburtstag*. Edited by Ulrich Hübner and Ernest Axel Knauf. OBO 186. Freiburg [Schweiz]: Universitätsverlag. Göttingen: Vandenhoeck & Ruprecht.

———. 2003. 'Chronology: A Skeleton without Flesh? Sennacherib's Campaign as a Case-Study'. Pages 46-72 in Grabbe 2003.

Ben-Ami, Doron. 2014. 'Notes on the Iron IIA Settlement in Jerusalem in Light of Excavations in the Northwest of the City of David'. *Tel Aviv* 41:3-19.

Biran, Avraham, and Joseph Naveh. 1993. 'An Aramaic Stele Fragment from Tel Dan'. *IEJ* 43:81-98.

Blenkinsopp, Joseph. 2013. *David Remembered: Kingship and National Identity in Ancient Israel*. Grand Rapids, MI: Eerdmans.

Bodner, Keith. 2012. *Jeroboam's Royal Drama*. Biblical Refigurations. Oxford: Oxford University Press.

Braun, Martin. 1938. *History and Romance in Graeco-Oriental Literature*, with a Preface by Prof. A.J. Toynbee. Oxford: Blackwell.

Bruce, I.A.F. 1967. *An Historical Commentary on the 'Hellenica Oxyrhynchia'*. Cambridge Classical Studies. Cambridge: Cambridge University Press.

Brueggemann, Walter. 2000. *1 and 2 Kings*. Smyth & Helwys Bible Commentary. Macon, GA: Smyth & Helwys.

Campbell, Antony F., S.J. 1986. *Of Prophets and Kings: A Late Ninth-Century Document (1 Samuel 1–2 Kings 10)*. CBQMS 17. Washington, DC: Catholic University of America.

Campbell, Anthony F., and Mark A. O'Brien. 2000. *Unfolding the Deuteronomistic History: Origins, Upgrades, Present Text*. Minneapolis: Fortress.

Childs, Brevard S. 1967. *Isaiah and the Assyrian Crisis*. Studies in Biblical Theology, Second Series 3. London: SCM.

———. 1970. *Biblical Theology in Crisis*. Philadelphia: Westminster.

Claburn, W.E. 1973. 'The Fiscal Basis of Josiah's Reforms'. *JBL* 92:11-22.

Cogan, Mordechai. 2001. *I Kings: A New Translation with Introduction and Commentary*. AB 10. Garden City, NY: Doubleday.

Cogan, Mordechai, and Hayim Tadmor. 1988. *II Kings: A New Translation with Introduction and Commentary*. AB 11. Garden City, NY: Doubleday.

Cohn, Robert L. 2000. *2 Kings*. Berit Olam. Collegeville, MN: Liturgical.

Cross, Frank Moore, et al., eds. 2005. *Discoveries in the Judaean Desert, Volume 17: Qumran Cave 4: XII 1–2 Samuel*. Oxford: Clarendon.

Davies, Philip R. 2005. 'Josiah and the Law Book'. Pages 65-77 in Grabbe 2005.

Day, John. 1985. *God's Conflict with the Dragon and the Sea*. Cambridge: Cambridge University Press.

Derow, Peter. 1994. 'Historical Explanation: Polybius and his Predecessors'. Pages 73-90 in *Greek Historiography*. Edited by Simon Hornblower. Oxford: Clarendon.

DeVries, Simon J. 1985. *1 Kings*. WBC 12. Waco, TX: Word.

Dines, Jennifer M. 2004. *The Septuagint*. Understanding the Bible and its World. London: T & T Clark International.

Dion, Paul E. 1988. 'Sennacherib's Expedition to Palestine'. *Bulletin of the Canadian Society of Biblical Literature* 48:3-25.

Dutcher-Walls, Patricia. 1996. *Narrative Art, Political Rhetoric: The Case of Athaliah and Joash*. JSOTSup 209. Sheffield: Sheffield Academic.

Exum, J. Cheryl. 1996. *Plotted, Shot, and Painted: Cultural Representations of Biblical Women*. JSOTSup 215. Gender, Culture, Theory 3. Sheffield Sheffield Academic.

Finkelstein, Israel. 1994. 'The Archaeology of the Days of Manasseh'. Pages 169-87 in *Scripture and Other Artifacts: Essays on the Bible and Archaeology in Honor of Philip J. King*. Edited by Michael D. Coogan, Cheryl J. Exum, and Lawrence E. Stager. Louisville, KY: Westminster John Knox.

———. 2002. 'The Campaign of Shoshenq I to Palestine: A Guide to the 10th Century BCE Polity'. *ZDPV* 118:109-35.

Finkelstein, Israel, Alexander Fantalkin, and Eliezer Piasetzky. 2008. 'Three Snapshots of the Iron IIa: The Northern Valleys, the Southern Steppe and Jerusalem'. Pages 32-44 in Grabbe 2008.

Finkelstein, Israel, and Neil Asher Silberman. 2001. *The Bible Unearthed: Archaeology's New Vision of Ancient Israel and the Origin of its Sacred Texts*. New York: Free Press.

Fried, Lisbeth E. 2002. 'The High Places (*BĀMÔT*) and the Reforms of Hezekiah and Josiah: An Archaeological Investigation'. *JAOS* 122:437-65.

Fritz, Volkmar. 2003. *1 & 2 Kings: A Continental Commentary*. Translated by Anselm Hagedorn. Minneapolis: Fortress.

Gallagher, W.R. 1999. *Sennacherib's Campaign to Judah*. SHCANE 18. Leiden: Brill.

Geva, Hillel. 2014. 'Jerusalem's Population in Antiquity: A Minimalist View'. *TA* 41:131–60.

Ghantous, Hadi. 2013. *The Elisha–Hazael Paradigm and the Kingdom of Israel: The Politics of God in Ancient Syria-Palestine*. Bible World. Durham: Acumen.

Glassner, Jean-Jacques. 2004. *Mesopotamian Chronicles*. Edited by Benjamin R. Foster. SBL Writings from the Ancient World 19. Atlanta: Society of Biblical Literature.

Grabbe, Lester L. 1987. 'Fundamentalism and Scholarship: The Case of Daniel'. Pages 133-52 in *Scripture: Method and Meaning: Essays Presented to Anthony Tyrrell Hanson for his Seventieth Birthday*. Edited by B.P. Thompson. Hull: Hull University Press.

———. 1995. *Priests, Prophets, Diviners, Sages: A Socio-historical Study of Religious Specialists in Ancient Israel*. Valley Forge, PA: Trinity Press International.

———. 2001. 'Who Were the First Real Historians? On the Origins of Critical Historiography'. Pages 156-81 in *Did Moses Speak Attic? Jewish Historiography and Scripture in the Hellenistic Period*. Edited by Lester L. Grabbe. JSOTSup 317. ESHM 3. Sheffield: Sheffield Academic.

———. ed. 2003. *'Like a Bird in a Cage': The Invasion of Sennacherib in 701 BCE*. JSOTSup 363 = ESHM 4. Sheffield: Sheffield Academic.

———. ed. 2005. *Good Kings and Bad Kings: The Kingdom of Judah in the Seventh Century BCE*. JSOTSup 393 = ESHM 5. London: T&T Clark International.

———. 2006. 'Mighty Oaks from (Genetically Manipulated?) Acorns Grow: The Chronicle of the Kings of Judah as a Source of the Deuteronomistic History'. Pages 154-73 in *Reflection and Refraction: Studies in Biblical Historiography in Honour of A. Graeme Auld*. Edited by R. Rezetko, T.H. Lim, and W.B. Aucker. VTSup 113. Leiden, Brill.

———, ed. 2007a. *Ahab Agonistes: The Rise and Fall of the Omri Dynasty*. JSOTSup 421. ESHM 6. London: T&T Clark.

———. 2007b. *Ancient Israel: What Do We Know and How Do We Know It?* London: T&T Clark International.

———, ed. 2008. *Israel in Transition: From Late Bronze II to Iron IIA (c. 1250–850 BCE)*. Vol. 1, *The Archaeology*. LHBOTS 491 = ESHM 7. London: T&T Clark International.

——— 2012. 'Omri and Son, Incorporated: The Business of History'. Pages 61-83 in *Congress Volume Helsinki 2010*. Edited by Martti Nissinen. VTSup 148. Leiden: Brill.

———. 2015. 'The Use and Abuse of Herodotus by Biblical Scholars'. Pages 49-72 in *Assessing Biblical and Classical Sources for the Reconstruction of Persian Influence, History and Culture*. Edited by Anne Fitzpatrick-McKinley. Classica et Orientalia 10. Wiesbaden: Harrassowitz, 2015.

————. 2016. 'The Mighty Men of Israel: 1–2 Samuel and History'. Pages 83-104 in *The Books of Samuel: Stories – History – Reception History*. Edited by Walter Dietrich, Cynthia Edenburg, and Philippe Hugo. Bibliotheca Ephemeridum Theologicarum Lovaniensium 284. Leuven: Peeters, 2016.

Gray, John. 1970. *I and II Kings*. 2nd ed. OTL. Philadelphia: Westminster.

Grayson, A. Kirk. 1975. *Assyrian and Babylonian Chronicles*. Texts from Cuneiform Sources 5. Locust Valley, NY: J.J. Augustin.

————. 1996. *Assyrian Rulers of the Early First Millennium BC II (858–745 BC)*. Royal Inscriptions of the Mesopotamia: Assyrian Periods 3. Toronto: University of Toronto Press.

Gross, Walter, ed. 1995. *Jeremia und die 'deuteronomistische Bewegung'*. BBB 98. Beltz: Athenäum.

Halpern, Baruch. 1988. *The First Historians: The Hebrew Bible and History*. San Francisco: Harper & Row.

Handy, Lowell K., ed. 1997. *The Age of Solomon: Scholarship at the Turn of the Millennium*. SHCANE 11. Leiden: Brill.

Haran, Menahem. 1999. 'The Books of the Chronicles "of the Kings of Judah" and "of the Kings of Israel": What Sort of Books Were They?'. *VT* 49:156-64.

Hardmeier, Christof. 2005. 'King Josiah in the Climax of DtrH (2 Kgs 22–23) and the Pre-Dtr Document of a Cult Reform at the Place of Residence (23.4-15*): Criticism of Sources, Reconstruction of Earlier Texts and the History of Theology of 2 Kgs 22–23'. Pages 123-63 in Grabbe 2005.

Herzog, Ze'ev. 2010. 'Perspectives on Southern Israel's Cult Centralization: Arad and Beer-sheba'. Pages 169-99 in *One God, One Cult, One Nation: Archaeological and Biblical Perspectives*. BZAW 405. Berlin: de Gruyter.

Hobbs, T.R. 1986. *2 Kings*. WBC 13/2. Waco, TX: Word.

Holladay, Steven W. 1992. 'Kings, Book of 1–2'. *ABD* 4:69-83.

Hornblower, Simon. 1987. *Thucydides*. Baltimore: Johns Hopkins University Press.

Huizinga, Johan. 1936. 'A Definition of the Concept of History'. Pages 1-10 in *Philosophy and History: Essays Presented to Ernst Cassirer*. Edited by Raymond Klibansky and H.J. Paton. Oxford: Clarendon.

Ilan, Tal. 2010. 'Huldah, the Deuteronomic Prophetess of the Book of Kings'. *Lectio Difficilior* 1. Online: www.lectio.unibe.ch/10_1/ilan.html (accessed 1 December 2014).

Jamieson-Drake, David W. 1991. *Scribes and Schools in Monarchic Judah: A Socio-Archeological Approach*. JSOTSup 109. Social World of Biblical Antiquity 9. Sheffield: Almond Press.

Jansen-Winkeln, Karl. 2006. 'II. 10 The Chronology of the Third Intermediate Period: Dyns. 22-24'. Pages 234-64 in *Ancient Egyptian Chronology*. Edited by Erik Hornung, Rolf Drauss, and David A. Warburton. HdO Section One, Volume 83. Leiden: Brill.

Jepsen, Alfred. 1956. *Die Quellen des Königsbuches*. 2nd ed. with Supplement. Halle: Max Niemeyer.

Jones, Gwilym H. 1984. *1 and 2 Kings*. 2 vols. NCB; London: Marshall, Morgan & Scott. Grand Rapids, MI: Eerdmans.

Killebrew, Ann E. 2003. 'Biblical Jerusalem: An Archaeological Assessment'. Pages 329-45 in Vaughn and Killebrew 2003.

Kitchen, K. A. 1997. 'Sheba and Arabia'. Pages 126-53 in Handy 1997.

Knauf, Ernst Axel. 1997. 'Le roi est mort, vive le roi! A Biblical Argument for the Historicity of Solomon'. Pages 81-95 in Handy 1997.

———. 2000. 'Does "Deuteronomistic Historiography" (DH) Exist?'. Pages 388-98 in de Pury, Römer, and Macchi 2000.

———. 2001. 'Hezekiah or Manasseh? A Reconsideration of the Siloam Tunnel and Inscription'. *TA* 28:281-87.

———. 2005. 'The Glorious Days of Manasseh'. Pages 164-88 in Grabbe 2005.

———. 2007. 'Was Omride Israel a Sovereign State?' Pages 100-103 in Grabbe 2007a.

———. 2008. 'From Archaeology to History, Bronze and Iron Ages with Special Regard to the Year 1200 BCE and the Tenth Century'. Pages 72-85 in Grabbe 2008.

König, Friedrich Wilhelm. 1972. *Die Persika des Ktesias von Knidos*. AfO Beiheft 18. Graz: Archiv für Orientforschung.

Kuan, Jeffrey Kah-jin. 1995. *Neo-Assyrian Historical Inscriptions and Syria-Palestine: Israelite/Judean-Tyrian-Damascene Political and Commercial Relations in the Ninth-Eighth Centuries BCE*. Jian Dao Dissertation Series 1 = Bible and Literature 1. Hong Kong: Alliance Bible Seminary.

Lipiński, Edward. 2000. *The Aramaeans: Their Ancient History, Culture, Religion*. OLA 100. Leuven: Peeters.

Lipschits, Oded. 2005. *The Fall and Rise of Jerusalem: Judah under Babylonian Rule*. Winona Lake, IN: Eisenbrauns.

Liverani, Mario. 2005. *Israel's History and the History of Israel*. Translated by Chiara Peri and Philip R. Davies. London: Equinox.

Lloyd, Alan B. 1988. *Herodotus Book II: Commentary 99-182*. Etudes préliminaires aux religions orientales dan l'Empire romain 43. Leiden: Brill.

Lohfink, Norbert. 1995. 'Gab es eine deuteronomistische Bewegung?'. Pages 313-82 in Gross 1995.

Long, Burke O. 1984. *1 Kings, with an Introduction to Historical Literature*. FOTL 9. Grand Rapids, MI: Eerdmans.

———. 1991. *2 Kings*. FOTL 10. Grand Rapids, MI: Eerdmans.

Maeir, Aren M., and Joe Uziel. 2007. 'A Tale of Two Tells: A Comparative Perspective on Tel Miqne-Ekron and Tell eṣ-Ṣâfî/Gath in Light of Recent Archaeological Research'. Pages 29-42 in *'Up to the Gates of Ekron': Essays on the Archaeology and History of the Eastern Mediterranean in Honor of Seymour Gitin*. Edited by S. Crawford, A. Ben-Tor, J.P. Dessel, W.G. Dever, A. Mazar and J. Aviram. Jerusalem: Israel Exploration Society.

Malamat, Abraham. 1982. 'A Political Look at the Kingdom of David and Solomon and its Relations with Egypt'. Pages 189-204 in *Studies in the Period of David and Solomon and Other Essays*. Edited by Tomoo Ishida. Winona Lake, IN: Eisenbrauns.

Mazar, Amihai. 2008. 'From 1200 to 850 BCE: Remarks on Some Selected Issues'. Pages 86-120 in Grabbe 2008.

Mazar, Eilat. 2011. *Discovering the Solomonic Wall in Jerusalem: A Remarkable Archaeological Adventure*. Jerusalem: Shoham Academic Research and Publication, 2011.

Miller, J. Maxwell. 1966. 'The Elisha Cycle and the Accounts of the Omride Wars'. *JBL* 85:441-54.

———. 1967. 'The Fall of the House of Ahab'. *VT* 17:307-24.

———. 1968. 'The Rest of the Acts of Jehoahaz (I KINGS 20 22$_{1-38}$)'. *ZAW* 80:337-72.

Miller, J. Maxwell, and John H. Hayes. 1986. *A History of Ancient Israel and Judah*. Minneapolis: Fortress. London: SCM.

Momigliano, Arnaldo D. 1966. 'Historiography on Written Tradition and Historiography on Oral Tradition'. Pages 211-20 in *Studies in Historiography*. London: Weidenfeld. New York: Harper & Row.

Montgomery, James A. 1951. *A Critical and Exegetical Commentary on the Books of Kings*. Edited by Henry Snyder Gehman. ICC. Edinburgh: T. & T. Clark.

Muller, Martin I. 1998. *1 Kings, Volume 1: 1 Kings 1–11*. Historical Commentary on the Old Testament. Leuven: Peeters.

Na'aman, Nadav. 1991. 'The Kingdom of Judah under Josiah'. *TA* 18:3-71.

———. 1994. 'Hezekiah and the Kings of Assyria'. *TA* 21:235-54.

———. 1995. 'The Debated Historicity of Hezekiah's Reform in the Light of Historical and Archaeological Research'. *ZAW* 107:179-95.

———. 1997. 'Sources and Composition in the History of Solomon'. Pages 57-80 in Handy 1997.

———. 1999. 'The Contribution of Royal Inscriptions for a Re-evaluation of the Book of Kings as a Historical Source'. *JSOT* 82:3-17.

———. 2002. 'The Abandonment of Cult Places in the Kingdom of Israel and Judah as Acts of Cult Reform'. *UF* 34:585-602.

———. 2003. 'La Bible à la croisée des sources'. *Annales: Histoire, Sciences Sociales* 58, no. 6 (Nov.–Dec.): 1321-46.

———. 2005a. 'The Sources Available for the Author of the Book of Kings'. Pages 99-114 in *Recenti tendenze nella ricostruzione della storia antica d'Israele*. Edited by Mario Liverani. Contributi del Centro Linceo Interdisciplinare 'Beniamino Segre' 110. Rome: Accademia Nazionale dei Lincei.

———. 2005b. 'The Kingdom of Judah under Josiah'. Pages 189-247 in Grabbe 2005.

Na'aman, Nadav, and Ran Zadok. 2000. 'Assyrian Deportations to the Province of Samerina in the Light of Two Cuneiform Tablets from Tell Hadid'. *TA* 27:159-88.

Nelson, R.D. 1981. *The Double Redaction of the Deuteronomistic History*. JSOTSup 18. Sheffield: JSOT.

Newsom, Carol A., and Sharon H. Ringe, eds. 1998. *Women's Bible Commentary: Expanded Edition*. Louisville, KY: Westminster John Knox. London: SPCK.

Niehr, Herbert. 1995. 'Die Reform des Joschija: Methodische, historische und religions-geschichtliche Aspekte'. Pages 33-55 in Gross 1995.

Niemann, Hermann Michael. 1997. 'The Socio-Political Shadow Cast by the Biblical Solomon'. Pages 252-99 in Handy 1997.

———. 2007. 'Royal Samaria—Capital or Residence? or: The Foundation of the City of Samaria by Sargon II'. Pages 184-207 in Grabbe 2007a.

Noth, Martin. 1943. *Überlieferungsgeschichtliche Studien: Die sammelnden und bear-beitenden Geschichtswerke im Alten Testament*. Schriften der Königsberger Gelehrten Gesellschaft, Geisteswissenschaftliche Klass 18. Jahr, Heft 2. Halle: Max Niemeyer.

———. 1960. *The History of Israel*. Revised translation. London: A. & C. Black. New York: Harper & Row. ET of *Geschichte Israels*. Göttingen: Vandenhoeck & Ruprecht, 1950.

———. 1968. *Könige I: Könige. Kapitel 1–16*. Biblischer Kommentar, Altes Testament 9/1. Neukirchen–Vluyn: Neukirchener Verlag.

———. 1981. *The Deuteronomistic History*. JSOTSup 15. Sheffield: JSOT, 1981. ET of Chapters 1–13.

O'Brien, Mark A. 1989. *The Deuteronomistic History Hypothesis: a Reassessment*. OBO 92. Freiburg [Schweiz]: Universitätsverlag. Göttingen: Vandenhoeck & Ruprecht.

Oded, Bustanay. 1979. *Mass Deportations and Deportees in the Neo-Assyrian Empire.* Wiesbaden: Reichert.

———. 2000. 'The Settlements of the Israelite and Judean Exiles in Mesopotamia in the 8th-6th Centuries BCE'. Pages 91-103 in *Studies in Historical Geography and Biblical Historiography Presented to Zecharia Kallai.* Edited by G. Galil and Moshe Weinfeld. VTSup 81. Leiden: Brill.

Parpola, Simo. 1980. 'The Murderer of Sennacherib'. Pages 161-70 in *Death in Mesopotamia: Papers Read at the XXVIe Rencontre assyriologique international.* Edited by B. Alster. MESOPOTAMIA: Copenhagen Studies in Assyriology 8. Copenhagen: Akademisk.

Paton, W.R. 1922–27. *Polybius, The Histories.* Cambridge, MA: Harvard University Press. London: Heinemann.

Perdue, Leo G., and Warren Carter. 2015. *Israel and Empire: A Postcolonial History of Israel and Early Judaism.* Edited by Coleman A. Baker. London: Bloomsbury T&T Clark.

Perry, Ben Edwin. 1967. *The Ancient Romances: A Literary-Historical Account of their Origins.* Berkeley: University of California Press.

Pitard, Wayne T. 1987. *Ancient Damascus: A Historical Study of the Syrian City-State from Earliest Times until its Fall to the Assyrians in 732 B.C.E.* Winona Lake, IN: Eisenbrauns.

Provan, Iain W. 1995. *1 and 2 Kings.* New international Bible Commentary. Peabody, MA: Hendrickson. Carlisle: Paternoster.

Pruin, Dagmar. 2006. *Geschichten und Geschichte: Isebel als historische und literarische Gestalt.* OBO 222. Freibourg: Universitäts Verlag; Göttingen: Vandenhoeck & Ruprecht.

———. 2007. 'What Is in a Text?—Searching for Jezebel'. Pages 208-35 in Grabbe 2007a.

Pury, Albert de, Thomas Römer, and Jean-Daniel Macchi, eds. 2000. *Israel Constructs its History: Deuteronomistic Historiography in Recent Research.* JSOTSup 306. Sheffield: Sheffield Academic.

Rad, Gerhard von. *Old Testament Theology.* 2 vols. New York: Harper & Row, 1962–65.

Rofé, Alexander. 1988. 'The Vineyard of Naboth: The Origin and Message of the Story'. *VT* 38:89-104.

Römer, Thomas C. 2005. *The So-Called Deuteronomistic History: A Sociological, Historical and Literary Introduction.* London: T&T Clark International.

Römer, Thomas C., and Albert de Pury. 2000. 'Römer, 'Deuteronomistic Historiography (DH): History of Research and Debated Issues'. Pages 24-141 in de Pury, Römer, and Macchi 2000.

Schipper, Bernd Ulrich. 1999. *Israel und Ägypten in der Königszeit: Die kulturellen Kontakte von Salomo bis zum Fall Jerusalems.* OBO 170. Freiburg [Schweiz]: Universitätsverlag. Göttingen: Vandenhoeck & Ruprecht.

Shea, William H. 1985. 'Sennacherib's Second Palestinian Campaign'. *JBL* 104:410-18.

Shortland, A.J. 2005. 'Shishak, King of Egypt: the Challenges of Egyptian Calendrical Chronology'. Pages 43-54 in *The Bible and Radiocarbon Dating: Archaeology, Text and Science.* Edited by Thomas E. Levy and Thomas Higham. London: Equinox.

Smith, Mark S. 2001. *The Origins of Biblical Monotheism: Israel's Polytheistic Background and the Ugaritic Texts.* Oxford: Oxford University Press.

———. 2002. *The Early History of God: Yahweh and the Other Deities in Ancient Israel.* 2nd ed. San Francisco: Harper.

Smith, Morton. 1971. *Palestinian Parties and Politics That Shaped the Old Testament.* New York: Columbia.

Soggin, J. Alberto. 1999. *An Introduction to the History of Israel and Judah.* 3rd ed. London: SCM. Valley Forge, PA: Trinity Press International.

Spengler, Oswald. 1926–28. *The Decline of the West.* 2 vols. New York: Knopf. ET of *Der Untergang des Abendlandes.* 2 vols. Munich: Beck, 1918–23.

Stade, Bernhard. 1986. 'Anmerkungen zu 2 Kö. 15-21'. *ZAW* 6:156-89.

Steiner, Margreet. 2001. 'Jerusalem in the Tenth and Seventh Centuries BCE: From Administrative Town to Commercial City'. Pages 280-88 in *Studies in the Archaeology of the Iron Age in Israel and Jordan.* Edited by Amihai Mazar. JSOTSup 331. Sheffield: Sheffield Academic.

———. 2003. 'The Evidence from Kenyon's Excavations in Jerusalem: A Response Essay'. Pages 347-63 in Vaughn and Killebrew 2003.

Sweeney, Marvin A. 2001. *King Josiah of Judah: The Lost Messiah of Israel.* Oxford: Oxford University Press.

———. 2007. *I & II Kings: A Commentary.* OTL. Louisville: Westminster John Knox.

Tadmor, Hayim. 1973. 'The Historical Inscriptions of Adad-Nirari III'. *Iraq* 35:141-50.

———. 1994. *The Inscriptions of Tiglath-Pileser III King of Assyria: Critical Edition, with Introductions, Translations and Commentary.* Jerusalem: Israel Academy of Sciences and Humanities).

Talshir, Zipora. 1993. *The Alternative Story of the Division of the Kingdom: 3 Kingdoms 12:24a-z.* Jerusalem Biblical Studies 6; Jerusalem: Simor.

Tatum, James. 1989. *Xenophon's Imperial Fiction: On* The Education of Cyrus. Princeton, NJ: Princeton University.

Tatum, Lynn. 2003. 'Jerusalem in Conflict: The Evidence for the Seventh-Century B.C.E. Religious Struggle over Jerusalem'. Pages 291-306 in Vaughn and Killebrew.

Thackeray, Henry St John. 1921. *The Septuagint and Jewish Worship: A Study in Origins.* Schweich Lectures. London: Oxford University Press for the British Academy.

Thiel, Winfried. 2000–2014. *Könige (1 Kön 17,1–21,29).* Biblischer Kommentar, Altes Testament 9/2. Neukirchen–Vluyn: Neukirchener Verlag. [issued in fascicles]

Thompson, Thomas L. 1992a. *Early History of the Israelite People: From the Written and Archaeological Sources.* SHANE 4. Leiden: Brill.

———. 1992b. 'Historiography, Israelite Historiography'. *ABD* 3:206-12.

Uehlinger, Christoph. 1995. 'Gab es eine joschijanische Kultreform? Plädoyer für ein begründetes Minimum'. Pages 57-89 in Gross 1995.

———. 2005. 'Was There a Cult Reform under King Josiah? The Case for a Well-Grounded Minimum'. Pages 279-316 in Grabbe 2005.

Ulrich, Eugene C., Jr. 1978. *The Qumran Text of Samuel and Josephus.* HSM 19. Missoula, MT: Scholars Press.

Ussishkin, David. 1988. 'The Date of the Judaean Shrine at Arad'. *IEJ* 38:142-57.

———. 2003. 'Jerusalem as a Royal and Cultic Center in the 10th–8th Centuries B.C.E.' Pages 529-38 in *Symbiosis, Symbolism, and the Power of the Past: Canaan, Ancient Israel, and their Neighbors from the Late Bronze Age through Roman Palaestina: Proceedings of the Centennial Symposium W. F. Albright Institute of Archaeological Research and the American Schools of Oriental Research Jerusalem, May 29–31, 2000.* Edited by William G. Dever and Seymour Gitin. Winona Lake, IN: Eisenbrauns.

———. 2008. 'The Date of the Philistine Settlement in the Coastal Plain: The View from Megiddo and Lachish'. Pages 203-16 in Grabbe 2008.

Van Keulen, Percy S.F. 1996. *Manasseh through the Eyes of the Deuteronomists: The Manasseh Account (2 Kings 21:1-18) and the Final Chapters of the Deuteronomistic History.* OTS 38. Leiden: Brill.

Van Seters, John. 1983. *In Search of History: Historiography in the Ancient World and the Origins of Biblical History.* New Haven: Yale University Press.

Vaughn, Andrew G., and Ann E. Killebrew, eds. 2003. *Jerusalem in Bible and Archaeology: The First Temple Period.* SBLSymS 18. Atlanta: Society of Biblical Literature.

Veyne, Paul. 1988. *Did the Greeks Believe in their Myths? An Essay on the Constitutive Imagination.* Translated by Paula Wissing. Chicago: University of Chicago Press.

Waddell, W.G. 1940. *Manetho.* LCL. London: Heinemann; Cambridge, MA: Harvard University Press.

Walsh, Jerome T. 1996. *1 Kings.* Berit Olam. Collegeville, MN: Liturgical Press.

Warner, Rex, trans. 1954. *Thucydides, History of the Peloponnesian War.* Penguin Classics. London: Penguin.

Wilson, Kevin A. 2005. *The Campaign of Pharaoh Shoshenq I into Palestine.* FAT 2/9. Tübingen: Mohr Siebeck.

Wiseman, Donald. 1958. 'Historical Records of Assyria and Babylon'. Pages 47-83 in *Documents from Old Testament Times.* Edited by D. Winton Thomas. New York: Nelson.

Wright, G. Ernest. 1950. *The Old Testament Against its Environment.* London: SCM.

———. 1952. *The God Who Acts.* London: SCM.

Würthwein, Ernst. 1977–84. *Die Bücher der Könige.* Das Alte Testament Deutsch 11/1-2. Göttingen: Vandenhoeck & Ruprecht.

Young, Robb Andrew. 2012. *Hezekiah in History and Tradition.* VTSup 155. Leiden: Brill.

Yurco, Frank J. 1991. 'The Shabaka-Shebitku Coregency and the Supposed Second Campaign of Sennacherib against Judah: A Critical Assessment'. *JBL* 110:35-45.

Zertal, Adam. 1989. 'The Wedge-Shaped Decorated Bowl and the Origin of the Samaritans'. *BASOR* 276:77-84.

Index of References

INDEX OF AUTHORS